DIVORCE & REMARRIAGE

GUY DUTY

BETHANY HOUSE
PUBLISHERS
MINNEAPOLIS, MINNESOTA 55438
A Division of Bethany Fellowship, Inc.

This edition, 1983

Bethany House Publishers
A Division of Bethany Fellowship, Inc.
6820 Auto Club Road, Minneapolis, Minnesota 55438

Printed in the United States of America

Foreword

This book represents many years of the author's careful study concerning the important and troublesome subject of divorce and remarriage. His textbook has been the Bible. Not everyone will agree with the author's interpretation of the Scriptures, but it will nevertheless provide study material for both those with broken marriages and for counsellors.

We know that devout people will do all they can to correct the mistakes and sins of the past, but in certain cases these errors cannot be corrected. What then shall be done? Is a marriage ever completely dissolved so that a person can again remarry on scriptural grounds? What about those divorced who have already remarried and who now wonder about their relationship? Many such are under condemnation. Then, too, others who have not thoroughly studied the subject have contributed to that condemnation, quickly and easily condemning others, though they themselves have no real understanding of this problem.

If this book will cause readers to search the Scriptures in humble dependence upon the Spirit of God to give light and help, we feel that this book has accomplished its purpose. It is therefore being sent to the public with the hope that marriage will be honored and the sanctity of the home preserved. We also hope those who find themselves already with a broken marriage will receive some guidance as to what should be done so to be sure of the peace and favor of God.

T. A. Hegre, President
Bethany Fellowship, Inc.

Publisher's Note to the 1983 Edition

It has come to our attention that some have taken the teachings of this book and interpreted them more broadly than Guy Duty would have intended. In the hope of minimizing this, we have carefully examined the entire text and made a few minor editorial adjustments in order to more clearly express his position, particularly in the light of the current situation concerning divorce.

Guy Duty went to be with his Lord in 1977. He certainly would have deplored today's soaring divorce statistics, particularly in the Church. We ask that this careful study of the Scriptures concerning divorce and remarriage be applied only within the narrow confines of Jesus' statement in Matthew 5 as Reverend Duty would have wished.

Preface

> He who answers a matter before he hears the facts, it is folly and shame to him. (Proverbs 18:13, *Amplified Old Testament.*)

> In the legitimate sense of the term, every interpreter of the Bible is prejudiced, i.e., is guided by certain principles which he holds antecedently to the work of interpretation. (*International Standard Bible Encyclopedia.*)

> He who judges without informing himself to the utmost that he is capable, cannot acquit himself of judging amiss. (John Locke.)

My thanks to the copyright owners for permission to quote the above statements, and to all the publishers who kindly gave me permission to quote their copyrighted material. These publishers are named at the places of quotation. I also received help from many other sources I searched during the 14 years I worked on this subject.

My appreciation goes to Professor John Murray of Westminster Seminary in Philadelphia who kindly gave me permission to quote from his book on divorce.

Mr. Elmer Miller, a veteran member of the New York Bar, and a keen Bible student, gave me valuable advice on the publication of my first book on divorce which has been used in the new edition.

For years it has been my delight to discuss the meaning of the Greek New Testament with Pastor Demosthenes Vlahakis of Brooklyn, New York. He gave me valuable help on some important points.

Miss Mary Kibbe, of Point of Rocks, Maryland, typed the final copies of the manuscript. This was much appreciated.

Contents

"Evidence is the basis of Justice"
Jeremy Bentham
(Works, Bowring's ed. VII, 384)

Statement of Purpose

The divorce controversy in the Christian world has been endless. Hundreds have written on the subject, and it has been debated by church councils for many centuries, but multitudes remain perplexed.

For more than 20 years I believed the teaching that forbids remarriage to the proven-innocent party in divorce. I was so saturated with this belief that I looked upon those who disagreed with me as being some sort of heretics.

One day about 14 years ago a fellow pastor called to ask my opinion about the right of the proven-innocent party to remarry. This pastor had some young people in his church who had been divorced and he was satisfied that they were truly innocent parties. Our denomination does not allow the right of remarriage to these people.

At the time my friend called, I had come around to the opinion that the Scriptures on divorce *could* be interpreted to mean that divorce for adultery allowed the right to remarriage, but I was unable to give any proof for this. I then began a study of the subject that has continued at times for 14 years.

It seems to me that we owe it to these divorced people to fully study this subject. Many make dogmatic statements who have never studied it. Without any proof for their doctrine of condemnation they condemn the proven-innocent who remarry.

A few weeks after I began my study of the subject, I submitted to my fellow pastor various arguments to prove that the Scriptures on divorce permitted the right to remarriage to the injured party. He was convinced that I had proved my case. He then arranged for me to speak on the subject to a group of ministers.

I had some anxiety about doing this because of what might happen to me in my denomination, but I took the view that truth is truth and that it should get first consideration. *Many* leaders and ministers believe as I do but are afraid to speak out. They let their divorced brothers and sisters in Christ suffer wrong rather than defend them.

When I spoke to the ministerial group, I had prepared a paper on the subject which they approved without a dissenting vote. I invited rebuttal but no one attempted it.

After this, to put my paper to a thorough test, copies were sent far and wide to ministers, church officials, Bible teachers and born-again lawyers who know their Bibles. I asked them to challenge the arguments, and again the response was beyond my expectation. It was my prayer that if I was in error that God would have it exposed because my soul recoiled in horror at the thought of leading anyone into sin.

It was then suggested that the treatise be printed, so with what time that could be taken from the duties of a busy city pastor, I prepared the manuscript for my first book on divorce that was printed about ten years ago.

Leaders in my denomination sent me unsolicited letters of approval after reading it, and schools of my denomination asked for copies to put in their libraries. Enthusiastic letters of approval were received from ministers of various denominations, editors, Bible school presidents, and Christian lawyers. So far as I know, every born-again lawyer who read the book was satisfied that I had proved my case, and some of them are excellent Bible students.

The divorce problem has no personal concern for me. I'm not divorced. But it is a serious problem in our churches, and we should have the courage to face it with a full and unprejudiced study. Many are afraid of an investigation of truth.

Unscriptural divorce is one of the great evils of our time. Many modern churches are as lax in their divorce laws as were the ancient Pharisees who allowed divorce for "every cause." We denounce and abhor this Hollywood kind of divorce.

I believe that rigid standards should be set up against all laxity in divorce and that we should keep strictly to the Scriptures and allow only what the Scriptures allow. Many church leaders are careful about their divorce laws, and we don't blame them for that. They have not been more careful than we.

Of particular concern is the practice of those denominations that do not allow their ministers to perform a ceremony for the proven-innocent in divorce, but they receive these divorced people into their membership if a minister of another denomination officiates.

A pastor I know had a couple in his church who desired to marry. One was divorced, and the pastor was satisfied that the person was truly the innocent party. He told them he could not marry them because of his denomination's position, but he sent them to another minister for the ceremony. He told the couple that he wanted them to come back to his church and remain as members. This pastor then told me, "That's the only hypocritical thing I ever did."

Those experienced in these matters know there

is much of this sort of thing in these no-remarriage denominations. And in many cases, where these divorced people are the most qualified to hold church offices, the fact that they are divorced is kept secret. I have been a little surprised sometimes to learn how often this is true. Many of these pastors know their position is worse than inconsistent but are in bondage to denominational tradition. They admit they feel hypocritcal about it but don't want to "get involved."

When my first book was published it met with some official resistance, but after some correspondence it was officially decided that further publication of it would be left to my own conscience.

It seemed strange to me that leaders would object to my defense of these proven-innocent divorced-remarried people whom they accept into their membership and whose money they gladly receive.

Many divorced-remarried persons in some of these churches suffer endless moral cruelty. They are accepted into the membership, admitted to the Holy Communion, but put under the moral penalty of not being allowed to sing in the choir, teach a Sunday school class, or perform other services in the church—which leaves them in the shadow of adultery. They are half-saint and half-adulterer.

It is not my purpose to try to change the official position of these divorce-but-no-remarriage denominations. The roots of tradition are deep, and it may be too late to pluck them up; but as they receive these divorced-remarried persons into their churches, they should take them in all the way and not leave them under the subtle suspicion of adultery. If God has fully accepted them into the "body of Christ" (Eph. 4:12), why should they not be fully accepted into the church body?

One sometimes finds himself tossed back and forth on the horns of a dilemma. Should he follow his denomination or defend what he can prove to be the truth? Should he sidestep a moral question that involves ever-growing numbers of possibly innocent people accused of adultery because they remarried? When a denomination forbids its ministers the right to perform a marriage for a proven-innocent party in divorce, but will accept this party into their churches if another minister officiates, what then?

I beseech my brethren to believe that I have gone through this long and laborious study only for the purpose to help all concerned. Strife and division are far from my mind. If anyone can refute what I have written, I will bless the hand that corrects me and gladly write a retraction.

Since my first book was published about ten years ago, I know of only two men who tried to refute it. They were reputed to be men of outstanding ability in the Scriptures. In my debates with them, they constantly evaded the difficulties that beset their doctrine. They refused to answer fair questions that would have exposed their errors. They were silent when their absurdities were proved. They ignored the evidence of proved facts, and if other Bible doctrines had to be defended with the same method of interpretation that they used for their no-remarriage teaching, then Christian doctrines would be in a sad state.

Does divorce for proven and unreconciled adultery dissolve marriage? This is the main question. If divorce for such adultery dissolves marriage, then there can be no question about remarriage. If it does not, then the right to remarriage must be denied.

People sometimes ask why the Bible is not more definite about the right to remarriage after divorce for adultery, and the answer is simple. In the Bible, the right to divorce carries with it the right to remarriage. Jesus approved the Jewish divorce that allowed remarriage, but He restricted this Jewish divorce law to the cause of fornication.

This book presents evidence to prove that biblical divorce signifies dissolution. Those who oppose this view claim that it does not mean dissolution. They say it means "separation," or non-dissolution. From the 4th century Latin fathers, this non-dissolution has been referred to as "separation from bed and board." The issue then is *dissolution* versus *non-dissolution*.

I take the position that divorce for adultery as granted by Jesus means the absolute cutting of the marriage bond. After such a divorce, the marriage is null, void. and dead. It's the same as though the adulterous mate had died. If dissolution can be proved, then there is no question about the right to remarriage, because our opponents deny remarriage on the ground of non-dissolution.

A dissolution-divorce was the only kind of divorce known to the Jews. and Jesus did not give the faintest hint of anything else. It was also the only kind of divorce known to the Greeks and Romans. The separation-divorce was not invented by Latin monks until several centuries after Christ.

The New Testament law of divorce and remarriage is strict. Compared to the 30 grounds for divorce in our 50 states, it is very strict. The ancient Jews allowed divorce and remarriage for "every cause." In our 50 states, it is much the same, from leprosy in Hawaii, to vagrancy in Missouri. to incompatibility in Alaska, to mental cruelty in California and other states.

Why did the New Testament Lawgiver throw out

all causes but the one cause of fornication? Why the severity of the new law? What philosophy of law was behind the drastic and sweeping change?

In Old Testament times, men were allowed to have multiple wives and concubines, and some of the greatest saints were born from these polygamous marriages. But with the New Testament law, a man can have only one wife, and if she is an adulteress and divorces him, then, if our non-dissolution friends are right, he cannot have even one.

We shall take the New Testament law of divorce and remarriage and deal with it by the evidence we have gathered. We shall work out from the premise that, for the cause of all sexual sin, Jesus approved the Jewish divorce that allowed remarriage.

We have learned from dealing with some persons on this subject that repetition is needed on some points, and we must go over them again and again. What is redundant to some is not to others. We must throw light on the subject from different angles. We hope this will not offend the intelligence of the more educated and that they will tolerate what may be needed for others.

We cannot possibly deal with all the problems and questions of some cases of divorce. This book is written for those cases where there is clear proof of guilt and innocence, and there are thousands of such cases.

(Note: the reader will find it helpful at this point to read the author's definition of "innocent party" on pages 127-129.)

From all the material I have gathered on this subject, I have cut away all but the most essential facts and have condensed and arranged the material so as to make it easy for the reader to follow. Study the facts. Read,

think, and read again. You may be surprised at what you
see.

I ask the reader to withhold his verdict until he has
read to the end. I refer frequently to rules of interpretation in the book and have summarized them in an appendix. The reader should first read this appendix. Then,
take a seat in the jury box and I will present the evidence
for dissolution.

2

Christ's Divorce Law
In Matthew 5:32

> It hath been said, Whosoever shall put away
> his wife, let him give her a writing of divorce-
> ment:
>
> But I say unto you, that whosoever shall put
> away his wife, saving for the cause of fornica-
> tion, causeth her to commit adultery: and
> whosoever shall marry her that is divorced com-
> mitteth adultery.

Jesus here referred to Israel's official divorce bill
used by the Jews for about 14 centuries. To understand this divorce question in the New Testament we
must know the history of divorce in the Old Testament. We must study a subject in the light of its
origin. We must know the life-situation in which the
subject originated. All authorities on interpretation both
in law and theology say we must begin at the beginning, so let's do that.

In Moses' time, as in other times, many Jews
were cruel to their wives, and because of their cruelty
and hardness of heart, God permitted divorce. These
cruel Jews divorced their wives for "every cause"
(Matt. 19:3). They divorced them for the most frivolous reasons: if she burnt his biscuits, or didn't
season his food right, or if he did not like her man-
ners, or if she was a poor housekeeper, "even if she

spoils a dish in cooking," "even if he finds a woman more handsome than she." Repudiation of the marriage at his whim and pleasure was at the center of Jewish divorce legislation (*Talmud*. Gittin. 9.10; *Josephus*, p. 134).

All a Jew had to do to divorce his wife was to give her the divorce bill in the presence of two witnesses. The marriage was then legally dissolved and both parties were free to remarry. This "writing of divorcement" is recorded in Deuteronomy 24:1-2.

> When a man hath taken a wife, and married her, and it come to pass that she find no favor in his eyes, because he hath found some uncleanness in her; then let him write her a bill of divorcement, and give it in her hand, and send her out of his house. And when she is departed out of his house, *she may go and be another man's wife.*

Some Hebrew grammarians have been uncertain about the meaning of "uncleanness" here. The Hebrew term is *ervah-dover*, and it had various interpretations in the Jewish *Talmud* in different centuries and in various countries. It is translated "obnoxious" and "unseemly" in the Jewish *Torah* and *Masoretic Text* (Jewish Pub. Society, 1962). The Hebrew word for "defiled" in verse 4 signifies "disqualified," and it implies ritual disqualification, not moral.

(I had some interesting correspondence with Jewish scholars on the meanings of these Hebrew words. One was a member of the official Jewish translation committee in America, and another was an expert in rabbinic law.)

Some argue that this "uncleanness" was immorality, but this could not be true because the unfaithful

Jewess was stoned to death. When the Jewish theologians brought the divorce dispute to Jesus, they argued from this Deuteronomic law that divorce was allowed for "every cause." Jesus conceded this, but explained that it was allowed for "hardness of heart" (Matt. 19:3–9). Jesus would not have said that this divorce was for hardness of heart if the woman had been immoral. This is proved by the fact that Jesus allowed divorce for fornication (Matt. 5:32; 19:9). Jewish scholars with whom I corresponded on this subject did not reply to this argument.

Dr. Alfred Edersheim said this uncleanness "included every kind of impropriety, such as going about with loose hair, spinning in the street, familiarily talking with men, ill-treating her husband's parents in his presence, brawling, that is, 'speaking to her husband so loudly that the neighbors could hear her in the adjoining house' (*Chethub* vii. 6), a general bad reputation, or the discovery of fraud before marriage" (*Sketches of Jewish Social Life*, pp. 157–158, Eerdmans Pub. Co., 1957).

We are here mainly concerned with the fact that the divorce dissolved the marriage and the woman could "go and be another man's wife." If the second husband divorced her, then the second marriage was dissolved and she was free to marry the third time; but God specified that she could not return to her "former husband" (Deut. 24:3–4). When the woman married the second time, she did not have two husbands because God spoke of the first as her *former* husband.

If the divorce did not dissolve the first marriage, then I can see no escape from the fact that God approved adultery in the second marriage and also the illegitimacy of children born in the second marriage.

If God's law of divorce is "separation," why did
He not command this woman to "remain unmarried"
instead of saying she could marry again?

Our opponent will remind us that this divorce was
allowed because of "hardness of heart." True, but
God could not have allowed an adulterous remarriage,
no matter what the cause of the divorce was. So, here
at the origin of divorce, the evidence is clear and strong
that biblical divorce signified the absolute dissolution
of marriage with the right to remarriage.

At the time Jesus uttered the words of His new
divorce law in Matthew 5:32, divorce was a flaming
issue throughout Palestine. This issue is known in
Jewish history as the Hillel-Shammai dispute. Hillel
and Shammai were two famous rabbis who were the
heads of rabbinical schools in Jerusalem. They lived
about a generation before Christ. Hillel had gained
recognition as a leading authority on Mosaic law.
Shammai also had attained to prominence as a teacher
of the law.

Hillel taught that a Jew could divorce his wife for
any cause whatever. Shammai held that divorce was
lawful only for the cause of fornication. This dispute,
debated up and down the land, was between the
every-cause of Hillel and the *one-cause* of Shammai.
Remember! it was not a dispute about remarriage but
only about the lawful cause of divorce that allowed
remarriage.

Denial of remarriage after divorce was unknown to
Jews. (See *Jewish Marriage Anthology*, Philip and
Hanna Goodman, p. 294, Jewish Publication Society,
1965.)

Dr. Alfred Edersheim, the world-recognized Jewish
New Testament authority, wrote:

On the question: What constituted lawful

grounds of divorce? the Schools were divided. All held that divorce was lawful, the only question being as to its grounds. (*The Life and Times of Jesus the Messiah*, V. 2, pp. 332–333, Eerdmans, 1953.)

If the reader will view this subject in the light of its historical circumstances, the fog of uncertainty will soon clear away.

The principle is, that most documents refer to the circumstances under which they were written, the court in interpreting them should be placed as nearly as possible in the same situation as the writer. (*Encyclopaedia Britannica*, Interpretation of Documents, V. 8, p. 912, 1959.)

Various authorities have written about the Hillel-Shammai dispute. E. A. Westermarck was an authority of such high rank that he is quoted by the *Encyclopaedia Britannica* in its article on marriage. He wrote:

Like Shammai and his school, Christ taught . . . that a man might put away his wife for fornication but for no other reason. (*The History of Human Marriage*, V. 3, p. 327, 1922, Macmillan Co.)

Two opposite opinions were held by the followers of Hillel and Shammai, the heads of antagonistic schools. . . . Between these contending parties the Pharisees desired to make our Lord give a decision. Matt. 19:3. (*Pulpit Commentary*, V. 34, p. 242, old edition.)

Thus modified (except for fornication), the Lord's teaching becomes similar to the stricter school of Jewish interpreters (Shammai). Thus,

He tacitly takes sides with the severer school of interpretation. (*Dictionary of Christ and the Gospels*, Editor, James Hastings, V. 1, p. 484, 1906.)

The temptation (Mt. 19:3) turned upon the dispute dividing the two great Rabbinical schools, the which (Hillel) held that a man might divorce his wife for any reason ... and the other (Shammai) that divorce was allowable only in case of unchastity. The querists would be anxious to know which side Jesus espoused. (*Word Studies in the New Testament*, Vincent, M. R., V. 1, p. 108, Eerdmans, 1957.)

But their (Pharisees) main object evidently was to involve Christ in controversy with some of the Rabbinic Schools. Mt. 19:3. (*The Life and Times of Jesus the Messiah*, Edersheim, Alfred, V. 2, p. 332, Eerdmans, 1953.)

This Hillel-Shammai history is recorded in many leading sources. Of special interest is the comment by the New Testament scholar, Professor A. T. Robertson, who quotes McNeile:

It cannot be supposed that Matthew wishes to represent Jesus as siding with the school of Shammai.

Professor Robertson replied:

Why not, if Shammai on this point agreed with Jesus. Those who deny Matthew's report are those who are opposed to remarriage at all. Jesus, by implication as in Matthew 5:31, does allow remarriage for the innocent party. (*Word Studies in the New Testament*, Robertson, A. T., V. 1, p. 155, Broadman Press, 1930.)

Jewish theologians agree with Gentile scholars on this point. They cite Matthew 5:32, 19:9 as agreeing with Shammai. (See *Universal Jewish Encyclopedia*, V. 3, p. 578, 1941, and *Jewish Encyclopedia*, V. 44, p. 625, 1916.) Roman Catholic scholars also agree with this. (See *Catholic Encyclopedia*, V. 5, p. 56, 1933.)

These historic facts support our interpretation of dissolution-divorce. There isn't a shadow of evidence in the historical circumstances to sustain the teaching that biblical divorce means "separation from bed and board." This is not a Bible term. It is not used in the Bible.

Every book I have read by non-dissolution authors (35 in *one* library) ignored these historical facts, and this is sufficient to justify our rejection of their teaching.

It is a conclusion of fact that Jesus, in deciding the divorce question, indirectly answered a dispute between rival groups. In the bitter disputes brought to Jesus for decision, it was not His main purpose to judge the controversies of contending parties, but in His statements of divine truths it was an incidental result that the weight of divine authority fell to one side of the disputants.

Jesus, as a Divine Court of Appeals, handed down clear and simple decisions to the moral questions brought to Him. They needed clearing and it was in the interests of the Jewish State for Messiah to do this.

The paying of taxes to Caesar was another hotly disputed question in Israel. The Pharisees and Herodians were divided on it. The Pharisees held that the Jews should not pay taxes to Rome, but the Herodians said they should. When the question was brought to

Jesus, His decision went to the Herodians. The Pharisees were wrong (Matt. 22:17–21).

The question of a resurrection from the dead was a cause of contention between the Pharisees and Sadducees. The latter taught that there was no resurrection. The Pharisees said there was. The Sadducees brought the question to Jesus, and His answer upheld the Pharisees. The Sadducees were in error.

On each of these questions, Jesus took their disputes to higher ground, but His answers indirectly supported one side. This was also true of the Hillel-Shammai question. The New Testament Legislator said that a Jew could not divorce his wife "except for fornication," and that is what Shammai said. "Jesus did not go beyond the principle laid down by Shammai" (Lange).

Divorce was widespread throughout Palestine when Christ uttered the words of Matthew 5:32 because the opinion of Hillel prevailed. The woman in John 4:1–30 was not an exceptional case. She had been married to five husbands and the man she was then living with was not her husband. Jesus seems to have given recognition to the legality of the fact that the woman had been married to "five husbands," but the man she was living with was "not thy husband" (v. 18). This was a clear distinction of marital status.

Multiple marriages were common in Palestine. This was also true of Jews living in the cities of the empire. Whether the divorce was obtained in a Jewish or Greek court, it was easy to get.

I have often wondered what the Lord did with these badly tangled cases. Some think they know what the Lord did in the case of the woman with five husbands, but all they have done is to *guess*—and perhaps unwisely. Where Scripture is silent, should we not also be? Is not the silence of Scripture on any subject significant?

Now that we have gathered the necessary historical information, we return to our interpretation of Messiah's divorce law in Matthew 5:32.

In this case of Matthew 5:32, our Lord shows that the man who divorces his wife for any cause except fornication *causes* her to commit adultery in remarriage. The Lord assumed that the woman would remarry. The reason the act is called adultery is that she becomes involved in sexual sin with another man while still the wife of the man who divorced her. The divorce did not dissolve the marriage. She was still his wife and he was still her husband. The woman did not have the right to remarriage, neither did her husband. Both sin if they remarry or enter into sexual relations with another. In this case an undissolved marriage is clearly in view. The divorce leaves the couple still married. The question of *dissolution* is at the heart of the whole matter.

If the husband puts away his wife for the cause of fornication, the case is different. The marriage is dissolved and the man is not involved in the sin that the woman commits. The emphasis in the prior case is the wrong that the husband does to his innocent wife by his *unjust* divorce action. His wife had not given him just cause to divorce her. Christ here stressed the wrong that the husband does to his wife in exposing her to the sin that she commits with another man.

Jesus, in His divorce law, used a decisive expression—"saving for the *cause* of fornication." The question of divorce and remarriage centers around these words. What do they mean? How shall we interpret them? There is only one safe and sure method, and that is by the rules that govern the interpretation of any other law.

Johann Bengel, master of Denkendorf Seminary (1713–41), was the author of the notable Greek work *Gnomon of the New Testament*, which has had "great influence on New Testament exposition to the present day." On the meaning of "cause" Bengel wrote:

> Adultery is a sufficient ground for divorce because it is an actual breaking of the marriage tie. The words, *saving for the cause,* etc., apply also to the second clause, *and whosoever marrieth,* etc.

> *For this cause,* logos, a cause; why anything may be rightly done. (*Gnomon of the New Testament,* V. 1, p. 115, 1860.)

The use of "cause" *logos*—"for which a thing may be *rightly done*—has the same meaning in ancient and modern times. Greeks today use this word when they think they have a just cause to take someone to court. The following standard authorities confirm Bengel's definition of "cause":

> *The Vocabulary of the Greek New Testament,* Moulton & Milligan, Eerdmans, p. 379, 1959.

> *A Greek-English Lexicon of the New Testament,* Arndt & Gingrich, University of Chicago Press, p. 479, 1957.

> *Thayer's Greek-English Lexicon of the New Testament,* p. 381.

> *The New Testament in Greek,* Westcott & Hort. Lexicon, pp. 113–114, Macmillan Co., 1953.

Messiah told the Jews they could not divorce their wives for the frivolous reason of burnt biscuits or oversalted soup. He threw out every cause but the one cause of fornication. Christ did not abolish *all* divorce, as some claim.

Non-dissolution teachers argue that Matthew 5:32 is "an isolated text" and must be understood in the light of Romans 7:1–3, but this is not true because the writing of Romans was about 25 years away. It is unlikely that these people ever heard Christ speak on divorce again. It was not necessary for them to hear Him speak on it again because His divorce law was a complete statement.

It appears that when Christ dismissed the multitudes who heard His Sermon on the Mount, any Jew in that crowd was free to go to a Jewish court and divorce an adulterous and unrepentant spouse with the writing of divorcement. (In this same discourse, Jesus recognized the jurisdiction of the Jewish courts—Matt. 5:25; Luke 12:58.)

We have seen that Jesus, in legislating "saving for the cause of fornication," established a *law of right* for the dissolution of marriage. Fornication was a just or right cause for dissolution. Would Jesus make it *right* for a man to divorce an adulterous wife and then make it *wrong* for him to remarry? What kind of law would that be which establishes a right but places a no-marriage penalty upon anyone who uses the right?

Christ did not perplex the people with His divorce law. He did not leave His divorce law in obscurity to be amplified into clearness by Paul 25 years later. For the rightful cause of fornication, Messiah approved the Jewish divorce which allowed remarriage. I leave it to the reader to judge if the point is proved.

3

The Jewish Writing of Divorcement

It hath been said, Whosoever shall put away
his wife, let him give her a *writing of divorcement*: But I say unto you, That whosoever shall
put away [how?] his wife, saving for the cause
of fornication, causeth her to commit adultery:
and whosoever shall marry her that is divorced
[*with what writing of divorcement?*] committeth adultery. (Matthew 5:31, 32.)

It is necessary that we learn something about this
"writing of divorcement" because it is connected with
Bible divorce and is a key factor to the right interpretation of what Bible divorce means. *What Jesus
legislated about divorce and remarriage is connected
with this official Jewish divorce certificate.*
We have seen that the Mosaic writing of divorcement cut the marriage bond so completely that the
woman was allowed to go and be another man's wife.

"...then let him write her a bill of divorcement, and give it in her hand, and send her
out of his house. And when she is departed out
of his house, *she may go and be another man's
wife.*" (Deuteronomy 24:1, 2.)

The divorcee, with the dissolution bill in her hand,
was at liberty to enter into a new marriage. The
divorce-writing was her "letter of freedom"—"document of release"—that permitted remarriage. There

no longer remained any matrimonial relation whatsoever between the two parties. It was the same as though they had never been married.

The rules require that we interpret this divorce bill in the light of its historical setting.

> What a term or word or expression literally means can be determined only from an inspection of the *culture* of the people who used it.... God's revelation is set in a historical context.... We may appeal to history. We may argue that such-and-such was the practice among the Jews at the time of Christ as witnessed by Rabbinal writings.
>
> All interpretations that do not measure up to these criteria must be rejected or at least held suspect. (*Protestant Biblical Interpretations*, Ramm, Bernard, pp. 96–97; 101–104; W. A. Wilde Co., 1956.)

Dr. Wilbur Smith, the widely recognized authority on Christian literature, said (see Preface) that Dr. Ramm's book on interpretation was the most satisfactory work published in this country the past 40 years. And he predicted it will be the accepted text for hermeneutical studies in the conservative schools and seminaries of America.

I can name a hundred books on interpretation by both biblical and legal authorities who insist on the same interpretive principles as stated by Dr. Ramm.

It may interest you to see a copy of this writing of divorcement. The famous Rabbi Maimonides and other Jewish sources have recorded it. It was an ancient document when Maimonides recorded it (12th century). The divorce bill was defined with such clarity and precision that it even specified the river near

which the divorcing parties lived. And the Jews were
so zealous to keep everything Jewish that the bill was
invalid if prepared in a Gentile court.

In law courts, an original document, or an au-
thenticated copy, is "best evidence," because it helps
to establish the validity of facts and eliminates doubt
and misinterpretation (*McCormick on Evidence*, pp.
408–415, West Pub. Co., 1954; *Wigmore on Evidence*,
p. 219, Foundation Press, 1935).

For 14 centuries—from Moses to Christ—this divorce bill that allowed remarriage was the one and
only divorce of the Jews. It was to this bill and its
divorce history that Jesus referred in Matthew 5:31–
32. Dr. Edersheim said the bill "had to be couched in
explicit terms" (*Sketches of Jewish Life*, p. 158).
"They were zealous to have the bill in due form that
the woman might be able to show she was free to
marry again" (*Expositors Greek Testament*, V. 1,
p. 109). Oral divorce was allowed by heathen nations.

The importance of this bill is seen in the following
copy of it.

> On____day of the week____day of the month
> ____in the year____I who am also called son
> of____of the city of____by the river of____do
> hereby consent with my own will. being under
> no restraint. and I do hereby release, send away.
> and put aside thee. my wife____who is also
> called daughter of____who is this day in the
> city of____by the river of____who have been
> my wife for some time past! and thus I do
> release thee. and send thee away and put thee
> aside that thou mayest have permission and
> control over thyself to go to be married to any
> man that thou mayest desire; and that no man
> shall hinder thee from this day forward, and

thou art permitted to any man, and this shall
be unto thee from me a bill of dismissal, a
document of release, and a letter of freedom,
according to the law of Moses and Israel.

‗‗‗‗‗‗‗‗the son of‗‗‗‗‗‗‗‗Witness
‗‗‗‗‗‗‗‗the son of‗‗‗‗‗‗‗‗Witness
(See *Jewish Encyclopedias*)

This documentary evidence is another link in our
chain of proof. It shows that *Jesus was speaking about
marriage as dissolved by the writing of divorcement,
and not as dissolved by death.*

This bill or writing of divorcement implied,
not only a mere separation from bed and board,
as some restrict it, but a complete severance of
the marriage tie. (*Pulpit Commentary*, Mark,
V. 2, p. 95, old edition.)

It is a fact that Jesus authorized a divorce for
fornication, and what we want to know is: *What kind
of divorce* did He authorize? By all the facts and circumstances of the case, there can be only one answer:
Jesus, for the cause of fornication, approved the Jewish
divorce.

Jesus did not introduce a *new kind* of divorce. He
did not abolish *all* divorce. He corrected the abuse of
the divorce privilege, but approved the right use of it.
If He had intended to change the divorce bill to a
separation bill, why didn't He explain the change?
The separation-interpreters have torn this question from
its historical connections, and this is a major error.

The meaning of the maker of an instrument is
to be taken from what is contained therein and
also from what may be fairly implied by custom or the like. (*Encyclopedia Americana*,
V. 15, p. 265, 1958.)

In determining matters of fact, after the lapse
of considerable time, documentary evidence is
allowed greater weight than oral testimony.
(*Systematic Theology*, p. 70, Augustus Strong,
1899, Judson Press.)

Joseph's Intention To Use the Writing of Divorcement

Then Joseph her *husband,* being a *just* man,
and not willing to make her a public example,
was minded to *put her away* privily. (Matthew
1:19.)

We see now an illustration of what I mean by
the *right* use of the divorce bill. For centuries, "just"
(righteous) men had used the bill to dissolve their
marriages to unfaithful wives.

The privy divorce was a merciful provision to spare
an adulterous wife the shame and disgrace of a public
trial in the Jewish courts. When a Jew placed the bill
in the woman's hand in the presence of two witnesses,
the union was then officially recognized as dissolved.

The Jewish betrothal was more binding than our
"engagement" (Gen. 24:53–67). "Among Arabs today
it is the only legal ceremony connected with marriage." The text says that Joseph was Mary's "husband," and the angel spoke of Mary as Joseph's
"wife." Edersheim, writing about the Jewish betrothal, said:

From that moment Mary was the betrothed wife
of Joseph; their relationship as sacred as if they
had already been wedded. Any breach of it
would be treated as adultery; nor could the band
be dissolved except, as after marriage, by regular
divorce. (*Life and Times of Jesus the Messiah,*
V. 1, p. 150, Eerdmans, 1953.)

A betrothed Jew was forbidden to marry another woman until the bond was dissolved by the divorce bill. If he died during the betrothal, his espoused wife inherited his estate.

Under Mosaic law, marriage was held so sacred that both the betrothed bride and adulterous wife were put to death for unfaithfulness. And the reason for the death sentence was "to put away evil from among you" (Deut. 22:23–24).

Sometime after Moses, merciful Jews abolished the death penalty for adultery and substituted the divorce bill. Divorce would have been merciful for the adulterers and adulteresses killed in Moses' time.

I tried to find at what exact time in Jewish history the death penalty was abolished and the divorce bill substituted for it, but I could not learn this, not even with the help of the chief librarian of the Jewish division of the New York Public Library. The Jewish *Talmud* says the death penalty was abolished "forty years before the destruction of the Temple" (A.D. 70), but there are biblical facts to show that it was removed long before this.

When Joseph found Mary pregnant, he thought she had been unfaithful and he planned to divorce her with the writing of divorcement, and the Holy Spirit said he was a "just man" in this purpose. He was not a "hardness of heart" Jew like those who tempted Christ with their question about divorce for "every cause" (Matt. 19:9).

We have now seen evidence that the writing of divorcement could be used righteously. Joseph, a just man, intended to use the Mosaic writing. And, *the Holy Spirit, in the New Testament, states that Joseph was a righteous man when he intended to use this divorce bill to dissolve his marital bond with Mary.*

And, what was *just* in Matthew 1:19 would not be *unjust* in Matthew 5:32; 19:9. What righteous men had done for centuries, in both betrothal and completed marriage, would continue to be righteous.

Dean Farrar worked for 20 years on his book, *The History of Interpretation.* He wrote (Preface) that every interpretation that violated the *grammatical-historical method* of hermeneutics was an "autocratic manipulation," and an "exegetic fraud."

Let the *rule of custom* be admitted into this case and the theological fog surrounding it will vanish. "Custom is the making of a law." (Quoted in *Black's Law Dictionary*, p. 461, West Pub. Co., 4th edition, 1957.)

While doing research on this subject I found many biblical scholars who frankly admitted their doubt about the meaning of Christ's divorce law, including some Roman Catholic theologians. They will remain in doubt about it unless they understand it as did the Jews who heard Christ utter the words. Will the reader accept the rule that: *"We may argue that such-and-such was the practice among the Jews at the time of Christ as witnessed by Rabbinical writings"*? If not, why?

I have quoted various sources that support the rules by which we interpret the divorce texts, and shall quote more as we proceed. My purpose for this is to draw from a wide range of authorities. This will require repetition but if I fail to do it some will doubtless say that I selected only a few sources favorable to my thesis. My experiences on this subject have taught me the need for this, so I ask the reader to be patient with it.

4

Does "Put Away" Mean Dissolution?

Whosoever shall put away his wife .... (Matthew 5:32; 19:9.)

Does *put away* mean dissolution or separation? The legal term "put away" had a grammatical history that always signified the absolute dissolution of marriage with the right to remarriage. The idea of a separation was never connected with it. I remind the reader that in courts of law, lexicons and concordances are considered superior evidence. So, I list below 12 leading Hebrew and Greek sources to prove the definition of put away.

Read any book by those with the opposite view on divorce and you will see that not one of them has quoted a Hebrew or Greek authority on the teaching that divorce means "separation from bed and board." There is none. Every lexicon I have searched has the same meaning of dissolution.

In all Jewish divorce history, divorce was called "a cutting off." The Mosaic divorce bill was called by the Jews *A Bill of Cutting Off*. The Hebrew word for divorce (put away) is *kerithuth* and signifies "a cutting off." This can be verified in:

Gesenius Hebrew & Chaldee Lexicon

Student's Hebrew Lexicon, Davies & Mitchell

Hebrew & English Lexicon of the Old Testament, Brown, Driver, Briggs

Bagster's Analytical Hebrew & Chaldee Lexicon

Young's Analytical Concordance

Strong's Concordance

The Greek word for divorce (put away) in the New Testament is *apoluo*. It is the exact equivalent of the Old Testament *kerithuth,* and it has the same precise meaning of absolute dissolution. It signifies:

"To set free; to loose; liberate; radically dissolved; cut loose, as a ship at its launching; discharge, as a soldier from the Army; undo a bond; cut apart; to cause all obligation and responsibility to cease; to sever; to free, as a captive, i.e., to loose his bonds and give him liberty to depart." See:

A Manual Greek-Lexicon of the New Testament, Abbott-Smith

The New Testament in Greek, Lexicon, Westcott & Hort, 1953

Vine's Expository Dictionary of New Testament Words

A Greek-English Lexicon, Liddell & Scott

The Vocabulary of the Greek New Testament, Moulton & Milligan

Among the early church fathers, "put away" (apoluo) was used in the sense of: "Set free, release, of death," "get rid of," "break up," "detached from" (*A Patristic Greek Lexicon,* V. 1, p. 201, Oxford University Press, 1961).

The primary meaning of the Greek *apoluo* is "to set free." An example is in Mark 15:6–15. "Barabbas lay bound" in a Roman prison, but "Pilate, willing to content the people, *released* (apelusen) Barabbas. . . ." This bound-released idea is the same in marriage and divorce as expressed by "put away." The power of a Roman governor set Barabbas free. The prison doors opened, his chains were loosed, and the prisoner was free. So also in marriage and divorce. In a Christ-authorized divorce, the wedding chain is broken and the nuptial captive is released. The marriage law has no further claim on the one released, as the Roman law had no further claim on Barabbas.

The lexical proofs for dissolution are unanimous and convincing. The definitions of Bible words have far-reaching importance because many Bible doctrines are expressed in a single word or term. When anyone changes the meaning of the word, he changes the meaning of the doctrine. Many false doctrines were made when teachers changed the meanings of sin, repentance, faith, salvation, grace, redemption, damnation, et cetera. Mary Baker Eddy changed the meaning of "sin," Fosdick changed the meaning of "damnation," and a prominent Episcopal bishop has changed the meaning of "conceived . . . of the Holy Ghost" (Matt. 1:20).

If our opponents are allowed to change the meaning of put away, then "we cannot deny the same privilege to others who may twist other passages in like manner." And if this is allowed, where shall it end? And who shall decide what may be changed and what may not?

The change of a single word . . . is often found to throw an entirely new shade of meaning over the Scriptures. (*Young's Literal Translation of the Bible*, Preface.)

Professor A. T. Robertson, the foremost Greek

scholar of modern times, spent 12 years on his greatest work, from which I quote:

> No more helpful remark can be made ... than
> to insist on the importance of the student's see-
> ing the original form and import of each word.
> (*A Grammar of the Greek New Testament in
> the Light of Historical Research*, Broadman
> Press, p. 143.)

Martin Luther, a master interpreter of Scripture,
knew, as all students of doctrinal history know, that
the dangerous errors of the church were distortions of
biblical words. This was true from the Council of Nice
(324 A.D.) to the Council of Trent (1545–1563), when
the great doctrinal debates of the theologians were a
"strife about words." Luther said:

> I have observed this, that all heresies and errors
> have originated ... from neglecting the simple
> words of Scripture. (Quoted in the *History of
> Interpretation*, Farrar, F. W., p. 327, Baker,
> 1961.)

When the importance of this word-history is realized, you may agree that I am not stressing this point
too much. The deadliest errors of Christendom were
made when men changed the meaning of "born again"
and "Son of God." Paul, in establishing his doctrine
of Christ, based it on the difference between the sin-
gular and plural of a single word (Gal. 3:16).

> It is noteworthy that the New Testament writ-
> ers and the Lord Jesus Himself did not hesitate
> on occasion to base their whole argumentation
> upon one single word of Old Testament Scrip-
> ture. (*Revelation and the Bible*, p. 139, Editor,
> Carl F. H. Henry, Baker Book House, 1958.)

Jesus, in stating His divorce law, did not leave us to guess at a moral riddle. He did not give us the choice between two possible meanings. If His meaning was doubtful, how can He "judge the world in righteousness"? (Acts 17:31).

Doubtful words will be construed most strongly against the party using them. (*Black's Law Dictionary*, p. 105, West Pub. Co., 1957.)

In the Appendix, I quote Dean Alford: "We must not violate the known usage of a word, and substitute another for which there is no *precedent*." Every precedent in the Bible meant dissolution. The concordances list divorce with the same meaning of dissolution in Deuteronomy 24:1; Matthew 1:19; 5:32; 19:9.

The U.S. Supreme Court has handed down historic decisions that were based on the meaning of one or two words in the Constitution. (See *Handbook on the Law of Evidence*, Tracy, J. E., pp. 350–354, Prentice-Hall, 1952.) Insurance companies have learned to include in their policies a section on definitions to prevent any misunderstanding about how the language of the policy is to be understood.

Jesus would not have used "put away" if He meant "separation." He took the same legal term *put away* that Moses used in his divorce law and incorporated it in the New Testament law. Jesus was always clear on a moral question. If He were introducing a new meaning to "put away," He would have carefully explained this vastly important point. Any wise lawgiver would have done the same.

Moreover, it is contended that, when He spoke about divorce, our Lord must have had in mind the complete severance of the marriage bond, since that was the only meaning His hearers could possibly attach to the word. (*Encyclopedia of Religion and Ethics*, V. 8, p. 438, Editor, James Hastings, Scribners, 1951.)

Twelve leading Hebrew and Greek lexicons define "put away" as dissolution. Not a single authority can be named for separation.

We conclude it is safe to say that the first-century New Testament reader understood "put away" to mean the absolute sense of dissolution with the right to remarriage.

Archbishop R. C. Trench of England (1807–1886), famous for his scientific study of languages, said that the failure to distinguish between word meanings was "the mother of all error." He also wrote about "the devil's falsehoods which lurk in words" (Suplee's *Trench on Words*, pp. 115, 339). Jeremy Bentham, the British legal authority, said that "a fallacy may lurk in a single word." Here is another cited in *The World of Law* (V. 2, p. 684, Piero Calamandrei, Simon & Shuster, 1960): "A single word ... may bring down the whole edifice."

What did "put away" mean to Matthew? What did it mean to the first-century readers of his Gospel?

But the object of interpretation is to get at the meaning of the person who *did* write the document. His words were not ambiguous to *him;* for he had a definite sense attributed to those words, and the judge's task is to find out what it was. (*Wigmore on Evidence*, p. 524, Foundation Press, Inc., 1935, his italics.)

Why all this argument and repetition about words? Because it is the crux of the whole matter.

"Except It Be for Fornication"

> Whosoever shall put away his wife, *except*
> it be for fornication.... (Matthew 19:9.)

We established the biblical definition of "put away"
in Christ's divorce law, and we come now to do the
same with "except."

Far-reaching importance is attached to the meaning
of "except." The question of remarriage hangs on it.
Does it allow divorce but not remarriage? Theologians
have debated this question from the time of Augustine
who lived in the 5th century.

The Greek word for *except* in Matthew 5:32 (saving for the cause of) is "parektos." The equivalent of
parektos (*ei me*) is in Matthew 19:9. It signifies:

> "To take out; outside of; to exclude; to leave
> out; apart from."
> (*A Greek-English Lexicon of the New Testa-
> ment*, Arndt & Gingrich, p. 630.)
>
> (*The Vocabulary of the Greek New Testament*,
> Moulton & Milligan, p. 492.)
>
> (*Expository Dictionary of New Testament
> Words*, Vine, W. E., V. 2, pp. 56, 57, Aliphants,
> 1948.)
>
> (*Thayer's Greek-English Lexicon of the New
> Testament*, p. 487.)
>
> (*A Greek Lexicon of the Roman and Byzantine*

Periods, Sophocles, E. A., p. 855, Scribner's &
Sons, 1887.)

The word *except* has the same meaning in English
as in Greek. Our English word comes from the Latin
ex plus *capere,* meaning to "take out." Leading English dictionaries agree on this definition. I quote three.

> Except. To take or leave out from a number or
> whole. (*Webster's Third New International Dic-
> tionary,* Copyright 1961 by G. & C. Merriam
> Co., Publishers of the Merriam-Webster Dic-
> tionaries. Used by permission.)

> Except. To take out from a number or an ag-
> gregate under consideration. (*The New Century
> Dictionary,* Appleton-Century-Crofts, Inc. Used
> by permission.)

> *Except* emphasizes the idea of leaving out,
> keeping out, or even shutting out. (From *Thorn-
> dike-Barnhart High School Dictionary.* Copy-
> right 1957 by Scott, Foresman and Co., Chicago.
> Used by permission.)

It is of the highest importance to note that these
English dictionaries define "except" as excluding from
"a *number* or *whole*"—or from "*an aggregate under
consideration.*" This is its meaning in Greek. The leading legal sources give the same definition.

The law encyclopedia, *Words and Phrases,* a monumental work in 101 volumes, gives the universally
accepted legal meaning of *except:*

> The purpose of an exception . . . is to exclude
> the operation of certain words that would other-
> wise be included in them. . . . The word 'except'
> means to exclude from an enumeration, the

scope of statement or enactment . . . to leave out
of account or consideration. (V. 15A, p. 69,
West Pub. Co., 1950.)

The publishers of this encyclopedia, in a note
attached, told about the increasing importance of definitions in court decisions. They give 31 pages to the
meaning of except, with numerous legal citations to
show that court decisions are based on the above meaning of the word. Other legal authorities agree. See:

American Jurisprudence, V. 27, pp. 103–106,
Bancroft & Whitney Co., 1940.

Cyclopedic Law Dictionary, p. 411, 3rd edition,
Callahan & Co.

Black's Law Dictionary, p. 667, West Pub. Co.,
Fourth Edition, 1957.

We now have the Greek, English, and legal authorities in unanimous agreement that "except" signifies
to 'exclude from a number or whole'—'to leave out
of an aggregate under consideration'—'to exclude from
an enumeration, the scope of statement or enactment.'
It has the same sense in Apocryphal, Classical and
Papyri usage.

Professor M. M. Bryant, of Columbia University
in New York, made a study to see how "except" and
other words are interpreted by law courts in handing
down legal decisions. Professor Bryant put the result
of this study in a book from which I quote.

When a person hears the word "except" he immediately thinks of 'not including.' He assumes
that whatever is excepted is left out . . . the mind
has a mental picture of that signification. It is
that which comes to the forefront of conscious-

ness. (*English in the Law Courts. The Part
That Articles, Prepositions, and Conjunctions
Play in Legal Decisions*, Bryant, M. M.,
pp. 118–119. F. Unger Co., 1962.)

This author lists many citations to show how one
small word is often the determining factor in court
interpretations of deeds, wills, contracts, or any document. "Jesus noticed small points of language"
(Robertson).

. . . all responsible scholars, whether liberal or
orthodox, must take every word seriously if they
are to deal fairly with Scripture. (*Revelation
and the Bible*, p. 389, Editor, Carl F. H. Henry,
Baker Book House, 1960.)

Isn't it true that often you do not understand a
statement until the meaning of one word in it is
cleared up?

The New Testament Lawgiver knew the dangers
of misunderstanding and the hazards of uncertain
meaning. If there is any doubt about the meaning of
His divorce law, then He cannot in justice condemn
anyone who remarries after divorce for adultery.

In doubtful questions of interpretation, the doubt
goes in favor of the accused. (*The Theory of
Justice*, Rudolph Stammler, p. 408, Macmillan
Co., 1925.)

The words of the exception are to be construed
in favor of the grantee. (*Pope Legal Definitions*,
p. 497, Callahan & Co., 1919, 6141 N. Cicero
Ave., Chicago, Ill.)

In the winter of 1965, a press report said that one
of the cases to come before the U.S. Supreme Court

was whether a section of a certain act of Congress was "void because of vagueness."

Jesus was a master of speech. He had a marvelous ability to state a principle in one brief statement. He was unexcelled with the short sentence, and the clearness and force of His laws are models of clarity.

Did Jesus intend that the modifying phrase—except it be for fornication—include the remarriage? Or, does the exception allow only for divorce? If it can be proved that the exception covers both the divorce and the remarriage, then we have solved a great question. Let's take another look at this law.

> And I say unto you, Whosoever shall put away his wife, except it be for fornication, and shall marry another, committeth adultery: and whoso marrieth her which is put away doth commit adultery.

The argument of no-remarriage interpreters is that the exception does not extend to the clause "and whoso marrieth her which is put away doth commit adultery." I will try to prove to you that it does.

In the Greek sentence, as in the English, it does not matter which position in the sentence the exception takes. It can be at the beginning, middle, or end, and the meaning of the law remains the same. But the exception sounds better in the middle of the Greek sentence and it is the proper place for it to be. The exception can be removed from its usual position and placed in an unusual position in the sentence without changing its bearing on both clauses. On the *Position of Words in the Sentence*, see *A Grammar of the Greek New Testament in the Light of Historical Research*, A. T. Robertson, M.A., D.D., LL.D., Litt.D., p. 417.

We now demonstrate the meaning of *except*.

a. Whosoever shall put away his wife, *except it be for fornication,* and shall marry another, committeth adultery: and whoso marrieth her which is put away doth commit adultery. Matt. 19:9.

b. *Except it be for fornication,* whosoever shall put away his wife, and shall marry another, committeth adultery, and whoso marrieth her which is put away doth commit adultery.

c. Whosoever shall put away his wife, and shall marry another, committeth adultery; and whoso marrieth her which is put away doth commit adultery, *except it be for fornication.*

Among the world of Greek scholars, Professor A. T. Robertson is considered "the prince of modern Greek grammarians," and he held that the exception in Christ's divorce law included both the divorce and remarriage (*Word Pictures in the New Testament,* V. 1, p. 155). Many Greek scholars, both ancient and modern, agree with Professor Robertson. Bengel taught that the exception applied to both the divorce and remarriage (*Gnomon of the New Testament,* V. 1, p. 115, 1960).

Here's a quote from a source found in the reference sections of leading libraries.

It might be further argued that the words, except it be for fornication, affect the first clause, and that remarriage after divorce even on the ground of adultery is here prohibited. Matt. 19:9. But if this were intended, it surely would have been explicitly expressed and not left to be inferred. And such teaching would seem illogical, because, if adultery be held to have broken the marriage tie so effectually as to justify divorce, it must surely be held to leave the offended husband free to contract a new tie. (*Dictionary of Christ and the Gospels*, Editor, James Hastings, V. 1, p. 484, 1906.)

The evidence we have cited from the Hebrew, Greek, English, and legal sources are considered by legal authorities to be "superior evidence." We must interpret the New Testament divorce law by the rules that govern the interpretation of any other law. A glance at the concordance shows that hundreds of times God spoke of His commandments as "laws."

We have given sufficient evidence for our conclusion that both the divorce and remarriage are linked to the fornication exception. The respected *Weymouth's Translation* of Matthew 5:32 reads:

But I tell you that every man who puts away his wife, except on the ground of unchastity, causes her to commit adultery, and whoever marries her *when so* divorced commits adultery.

This translation gives the true sense of Christ's divorce law. Jesus said the remarriage of the divorced woman would be adulterous, except for fornication.

6

The Meaning of Fornication

And I say unto you, Whosoever shall put away his wife, except it be for *fornication*, and shall marry another, committeth adultery: and whoso marrieth her which is put away doth commit adultery. (Matthew 19:9.)

Some teachers claim that "fornication" in Matthew 5:32; 19:9 refers only to "premarital sin." They teach that one can divorce a mate for sexual sin committed before marriage but not for sin after marriage. As usual, they give no proof for their dogmatic statements. When a man has proof, he doesn't have to be dogmatic, all he has to do is to submit his evidence.

Many make a big issue over the meaning for fornication, so it is necessary that we fully study it. There are two nation-wide radio preachers who *say* that fornication means only premarital sin, and much trouble has been caused by such factless statements.

What are the *facts* about fornication?

Fornication and adultery are synonymous terms in the Scriptures and they are often interchangeable. This is also true of other Bible words like "soul" and "spirit," "kingdom of God" and "kingdom of heaven." The specific meaning is often determined by the context.

In Hebrew and Greek, the word fornication includes incest, sodomy, harlotry, perversion, and all sexual sin, both before and after marriage. We are not primarily concerned with the definition of fornication in modern English.

Our English word fornication comes from the Latin *fornix* and means "brothel." Literally, it means 'vault' or 'cell' where Roman harlots had their abodes. Our leading English dictionaries recognize the Hebrew and Greek meaning of fornication.

The Hebrew word for fornication is *zanah*. It is used:

"of a married woman, to commit adultery. Jer. 3:1." (*Student's Hebrew Lexicon*, Davies & Mitchell, p. 185, Kregel, 1957.)

In Amos 7:17, a married woman is a fornicatress, Zanah. (*Young's Analytical Concordance*, p. 452.)

"Fornication. Heb. Zanah, to commit adultery. Every form of unchastity is included in the term 'fornication.' Mt. 5:32." (*The International Standard Bible Encyclopedia*, Vol. 2, p. 746, Eerdmans Pub. Co., 1952.)

All the leading sources agree with this definition of the Hebrew *zanah*.

The Greek word for fornication is *porneia*. It signifies:

"In Mt. 5:32; 19:9, it stands for, or includes adultery." (*Expository Dictionary of New Testament Words*, Vine, W. E., Vol. 2, p. 125, 1948.)

Fornication. "Prostitution, unchastity, (Demos. Philo. 12 Patr.), of every kind of unlawful sexual intercourse . . . adultery appears as fornication (cf. Sir. 23:23). Hm. 4, 1.5. Of the sexual unfaithfulness of a married woman. Mt. 5:32; 19:9." (*A Greek-English Lexicon of the New Testament*, Arndt & Gingrich, p. 699, University of Chicago Press.)

"Fornication must be taken to mean sin, not only before marriage, but after it also, in a wider sense, as including adultery likewise." (*The New Testament for English Readers*, Alford, Dean, p. 33, Moody Press.)

"Porneia. a. prop. of illicit sexual intercourse in general. Demos. 403.27; 433.25 . . . All other interpretations of the term . . . are to be rejected." (*Thayer's Greek-English Lexicon*, p. 532.)

The *Expositors Greek Testament* is a leading Greek authority by 17 distinguished scholars. On the meaning of fornication, we read:

"What does porneia (fornication) mean? Schanz, a master as becomes a Catholic . . . decides that it means adultery committed by a married woman. Some, including Dollinger, think it means fornication committed before marriage. The prominent opinion, both ancient and modern, is that adopted by Schanz."

"The term *porneia* is to be taken in its proper sense and is not to be restricted to any one particular form. . . ." (V. 1, p. 110; V. 3, p. 351.)

Many more sources could be quoted which agree with what I have cited. One or two more should be sufficient. Vincent's *Word Studies in the New Testament* applies fornication to married men (V. 4, pp. 35–36). Greek scholars refer to *The Vocabulary of the Greek New Testament*, Moulton & Milligan, as the "final court of appeals," because it shows from the papyri and inscriptions how Bible words were used in the time of Bible writers. On the meaning of fornication (porneia), this work says:

"... applied to unlawful sexual intercourse generally." (p. 529, Eerdmans Pub. Co., 1959.)

Leading church fathers understood Matthew's fornication to include adultery and all sexual impurity, and they were well qualified to know its usage among ancient people.

Jews in Israel were put to death for acts of fornication, both before and after marriage. The death penalty was imposed upon married Jews for incest, sodomy, bestiality, and all forbidden sex acts (Lev. 20:11–21). All these were included in fornication as written in their law codes. It was in this sense that Jesus used the word fornication when He stated His divorce law to the Jews. As Jesus did not give the least indication that He changed the Old Testament meaning of the word, this was the only sense in which they could possibly understand it. The meaning of premarital-sin-only was never attached to the word.

Many probably do not know that Dr. R. H. Charles of England was one of the most learned biblical scholars, not only of the 20th century, but of all Christendom. His monumental works are in the reference sections of leading libraries. Greek authorities appeal to his scholarship.

Dr. Charles' book on divorce, *The Teaching of the New Testament on Divorce*, London, 1921, is one of the most learned expositions on divorce. He said, "Our Lord embraced the side of the Shammites..." (p. vii), and Shammai certainly did not teach that fornication has the exclusive sense of premarital sin. Dr. Charles also said:

The history of the word *porneia* (fornication) in Jewish writings has never to my knowledge been investigated, nor have its manifold meanings been definitely recognized. The peculiar history of porneia comes to the front most in Jewish and Christian writings, but the word was used of different sexual sins in classical Greek. Since this question is one of peculiar importance, I have dealt with it in a special chapter (see p. 91). From that chapter the conclusion is inevitable that porneia could be used of sexual sin in a generic sense, or of any specific sexual sin. (page 23.)

Much of the following information I owe to Dr. Charles.

In Numbers 25:1-2, the 23,000 of Israel, including the chiefs who committed sexual sin with the daughters of Moab, were not all unmarried. Here their sin is designated with the word *zanah* (fornication).

Paul, in I Corinthians 10:8, said: "Neither let *us* commit *fornication*, as some of them committed, and fell in one day three and twenty thousand." Paul here referred to married Israelites who committed fornication, and said to the married Corinthians, "Neither let *us* commit fornication." Did "us" mean only the unmarried?

Christ, in Revelation 2:14, refers to the same event of the married Jews committing sexual sin with the daughters of Moab, and He said they committed "fornication." So in this reference, Christ, who used "fornication" in Matthew 5:32; 19:9, also used it with reference to the sexual sin of the married.

In Amos 7:17, fornication (*zanah*) designates the sexual sin of a married woman. This is paralleled with Dio Cassius' account of Messalina, 60.30. From classical times, fornication included the sexual sin of a married woman. (See also II Kings 9:22, *Amplified Old Testament.*)

Porneia and its cognates are used of idolatrous worship in Ex. 34:16; II Chron. 21:11, 13; Isa. 1:21; Jer. 3:8; and frequently throughout Ezekiel, chapters 16, 23. The relation of God and Israel is represented as that of a marriage. The symbolic language is according to the literal. In Ezekiel 23, porneia and its cognates are used nearly 20 times of idolatry. Idolatry with heathen nations was frequently accompanied by sexual vice. Porneia and its cognates are often used of such worship, and this worship was not confined to the unmarried.

Herodotus says these rites of idolatrous worship were connected with infamous sexual excesses. See Revelation 2:20, where Christ spoke of Jezebel and her idolatrous worship and that she caused His "servants to commit *fornication.*" Jesus here again used fornication in relation to the married.

In Hosea 2:5, fornication is used of Hosea's wife. "Harlot" is *zanah.* The sexual abominations of the married in Sodom and Gomorrah are referred to in Jude 7 as "fornication."

In the Jewish Apocrypha and Pseudepigrapha, porneia and its cognates become generic terms for sexual vice, and they are used for specific sexual vices.

Porneia (fornication) is used of adultery in *Sirach* 23:23; *Testament of Judah* 18:2; *Testament of Dan* 5:6; *Testament of Issachar* 7:2; *Testament of Joseph* 3:8. In the *Testament of Levi,* 14:6, the high priests (almost without exception) were married men, and fornication was used of the sexual violations of both the married and unmarried. In the *Testament of Asher* 2:8, the same combination of sexual sin is referred to with porneia.

In early Christian literature, porneia and its cognates are used of sexual sin generally.

Hermas, *Mand.* 4:1, 5, used porneia of a married woman.

Tation, *Orat. 10*, used porneia of a married woman. Heracleon, quoted by Origen in *Joan.* 13:15, used porneia of the woman of Samaria. *Origen* likewise understands porneia in *Matthew* 14:27. Also, *Acts of Thomas* (ed. Bonnet), p. 42.

Basil, in *epistulae*, cxcix, *can.* 46, used porneia of the married.

Chrysostom (and he certainly knew Greek), in *Matt. Hom.* 17, used porneia of a wife.

Gregory Nazianzus, *Orat.* 37:8, used *porne* of an adulterous wife. He also used *pornos* of an adulterous husband, *epistulae*, cxcix. *can.* 21.

Justin Martyr, *Apol.* 1:27, used porneia of sodomy.

Numerous references for this view of fornication are given in the valuable lexical work, *A Patristic Greek Lexicon* (Oxford University Press, 1961). This lexicon says in V. 4, p. 1122: "Fornication. 5. of illicit intercourse committed by married people, hence including, or identified with adultery. Matt. 5:32:19:9 . . . Porneia is adultery." *Baker's Dictionary of Theology*, 1960. p. 228, is in full agreement with this definition of fornication.

Fornication (porneia) and its cognates are used in the same sense in the New Testament. Here the married man guilty of sexual sin is a fornicator, and the married woman is a fornicatress. In I Corinthians 5:1, Paul said that fornication was frequent among the Corinthians, and incest was specified. Who can say that only the unmarried were guilty of this? In II Corinthians 12:21, Paul said he would bewail *many* "who had committed fornication." Were these many offenders the unmarried only? In I Corinthians 5:9, 11, Paul commanded the Corinthians "not to company with fornicators." Could they company with adulterers? From these references it is evident that Paul, a learned Jewish scholar, used fornication by its established usage. So also did the other apostles.

In Acts 15:20, 29, the apostles wrote to the Gentiles to abstain from fornication. Mr. Elmer Miller, veteran member of the New York Bar, is a lawyer with much experience in the Scriptures. He made a study of divorce and wrote the following in his *Memorandum* about fornication in Acts 15:20, 29:

It would be ridiculous to suppose that in the first century, A.D., when illicit intercourse was commonly practiced among Gentiles, that *porneia* was used only in the sense of illicit sexual intercourse among unmarried persons. If this were the true sense in which porneia was used in these two passages, then we would have the first Church Council, by indirection, permitting illicit sexual intercourse among married people.

Dr. Charles summed up his exhaustive work on fornication with this statement:

From Classical times onwards, fornication includes the sexual sin of a married woman. It was used of sexual sin as a whole, and also of specific sexual sins. The context in which it appears determines the sense to be assigned to it. It follows that from the 4th century B.C. in

Greece and 200 B.C. among Greek-speaking
Jews down to 96 A.D., porneia and its cognates
were used not only of fornication but of practically every other specific sin, as well as of
all sexual sins taken collectively. (*The Teaching
of the New Testament on Divorce, Charles, R. H.,*
pp. 91–111, Williams & Norgate, London, 1921.)

It was understood in this sense by a long list of
Christendom's greatest scholars and translators:

Augustine, Lactantius, Clement, Aramaic Trans-
lations, Luther, Calvin, Grotius, Post-Nicene
Fathers, Gesenius, Edersheim, Rotherham, Vin-
cent, Morgan, Robertson, Strong, Knox, Wil-
liams, Phillips, Moffatt, Weymouth, Wuest,
Montgomery, Goodspeed, Amplified Translation,
Abbott-Smith, Westcott-Hort, Driver, Douay
Version, Wesley, Hastings, Cruden, Liddell-
Scott.

I could easily name *many* more, both ancient and
modern sources. Our leading English dictionaries recognize the biblical sense of fornication.

"Fornication. In the Bible, any unlawful intercourse, including adultery." (From *Webster's
New Twentieth Century Dictionary*, College
Edition, copyright 1962 by The World Publishing Co. Used by permission.)

"Fornication is sometimes, esp. in the Bible,
used to include all sexual intercourse except between husband and wife." (From *Webster's
Third New International Dictionary,* copyright
1961 by G. & C. Merriam Co., Publishers of
the Merriam-Webster Dictionaries. Used by permission.)

See also:

Britannica World Dictionary

Funk & Wagnall's New Standard Dictionary

The New Century Dictionary

A New English Dictionary, Oxford Press (10 vols.)

American College Standard Reference Dictionary

A New English Dictionary on Historical Principles, Oxford Press (20 vols.)

Dozens of Bible dictionaries and encyclopedias give the same meaning. The following are a few.

Westminster Dictionary of the Bible

Theological Word Book of the Bible

Kitto's Cyclopedia of Biblical Literature

Harper's Bible Dictionary

Fausset's Encyclopedia & Dictionary

Unger's Bible Dictionary

Hastings Dictionary of the Bible

The leading commentaries and critical Greek works are in agreement with the above sense of fornication in the Scriptures.

It happens frequently that married persons are convicted of sex crimes so shocking that the public and press are barred from the trial. They are crimes for which God ordered the death penalty under Moses. Does God now require His innocent saints to be one flesh with them? Can these offenders, after serving a prison term for their sex crimes, return and renew their one-flesh relation with their innocent mates who—on the premarital view—were forbidden to divorce them?

The premarital teachers say that if these crimes

had been committed before marriage, then the innocent could have divorced them; but because they were committed after marriage, the innocent must "cleave unto" them until the end of life.

One of the premarital teachers with whom I debated the meaning of fornication admitted that Christ's divorce law requires the innocent to be one flesh with convicted sex criminals. To be consistent, he had to admit it.

From all the evidence we have seen, this is what we get:

Whosoever shall put away his wife, except it be
for all sexual sin, and shall marry another,
committeth adultery.

Here "adultery" is qualified by the sin that is committed in the new marriage. There is more in the Scriptures about fornication and adultery, but our purpose has been to show that in Christ's divorce legislation, fornication does not bear the exclusive sense of premarital sin.

Our view of fornication is fully certified by the evidence from the Old Testament, New Testament, Hebrew lexicons, Greek lexicons, Jewish Apocrypha, Early Christian literature, Classical Greek, Rabbinic literature, the Papyri, both Eastern and Western church fathers, the Revisions, and all other authoritative sources. The premarital view has no authoritative support.

7

Christ's Divorce Law in Matthew 19:9

The Pharisees also came unto him, tempting
him. and saying unto him, Is it lawful for a
man to put away his wife for every cause?

We shall see here the question of divorce in a
different setting. There is considerable repetition in
the Bible about various subjects, and here the divine
Author presents the same subject under different circumstances. When a subject is repeated, and new details added to it, it is called the *law of recurrence.*
Although the subject is repeated. we shall see it from
a new angle and learn new things about it.

Here Christ met the Jewish theologians on the
issue of divorce. It was, as we have seen, the hotly
debated question between the rival Rabbinical schools
of Hillel and Shammai.

The subject matter of this Scripture was the lawfulness of the Mosaic divorce for "every cause." These
Jewish scholars were able and clever men. They
wanted to know if it was *lawful* for a Jew to divorce
his wife for all the trivial causes that their famous
Rabbi Hillel allowed. *They did not mention remarriage
because that was not the point at issue.* There was
never any question about this. It was allowed by both
Hillel and Shammai.

Let's keep in mind that the subject under consideration in this passage was the lawfulness of the
Mosaic divorce law.

The exponents of separation-divorce use the *rule*

of subject-matter on other Bible questions, so we shall follow their example and use it on this question.

In the Appendix, I quote Charles G. Finney on rules of interpretation. He, a lawyer and theologian, used the same rules of interpretation on the Scriptures that I am using. He wrote:

> Language is to be interpreted according to the subject matter of discourse. (*Systematic Theology*, p. 241, Colporter Kemp.)

"Subject matter" means *"The subject, or matter presented for consideration; the thing in dispute"* (*Black's Law Dictionary*, p. 1594, Fourth Edition, West Pub. Co., 1957).

We now examine the subject "presented for consideration" to Christ, and shall see how He answered "the thing in dispute." Below we place in parallel columns the records of Matthew and Mark so you can see why leading scholars like Edersheim, Vincent, Alford, and many others say that Matthew "more fully reports," and that he has "highest rank in the accounts," while Mark's record is in a "condensed form." We italicize the part of Matthew's record that Mark omits.

Matthew 19	*Mark 10*
3. The Pharisees also came unto him, tempting him, and saying unto him, Is it lawful for a man to put away his wife for *every cause?*	2. And the Pharisees came unto him, and asked him, Is it lawful for a man to put away his wife? tempting him.
4. And he answered and said unto them, Have ye	3. And he answered and said unto them, What did Moses command you?

not read, that he which made them at the beginning made them male and female,

5. And said, For this cause shall a man leave father and mother and shall cleave to his wife: and they twain shall be one flesh?

6. Wherefore they are no more twain but one flesh. What therefore God hath joined together, let not man put asunder.

7. They say unto him, Why did Moses then command to give a writing of divorcement, and to put her away?

8. He saith unto them, Moses because of the hardness of your hearts suffered you to put away your wives: but from the beginning it was not so.

9. And I say unto you, Whosoever shall put away his wife, *except it be for fornication*, and shall marry another, committeth adultery: and whoso

4. And they said, Moses suffered to write a bill of divorcement, and to put her away.

5. And Jesus answered and said unto them, For the hardness of your heart he wrote you this precept.

6. But from the beginning of the creation God made them male and female.

7. For this cause shall a man leave his father and mother and cleave to his wife.

8. And they twain shall be one flesh: so then they are no more twain, but one flesh.

9. What therefore God hath joined together, let not man put asunder.

10. And in the house his disciples asked him again of the same matter.

11. And he saith unto them, Whosoever shall put away his wife, and marry another, committeth adultery against her.

12. And if a woman shall

marrieth her which is put
away doth commit adul-
tery.

put away her husband,
and be married to another,
she committeth adultery.

10. *His disciples say unto
him, If the case of the
man be so with his wife,
it is not good to marry.*

11. *But he said unto them,
All men cannot receive
this saying, save they to
whom it is given.*

12. *For there are some
eunuchs, which were so
born from their mother's
womb: and there are
some eunuchs which were
made eunuchs of men:
and there be eunuchs,
which have made them-
selves eunuchs for the
kingdom of heaven's sake.
He that is able to receive
it, let him receive it.*

We first establish the point that Christ and His
Jewish tempters understood "lawful" with the same
precise meaning. Many times, Jesus, the Jews, and
the apostles discussed points of Jewish law, and always
with the same vocabulary. On another occasion, when
the word "lawful" was used, both Jesus and the Pharisees understood it in the same sense. They asked Jesus:
"Is it *lawful* to heal on the sabbath?" Jesus replied:
"It is *lawful* to do well on the sabbath" (Matt. 12:10–
12). At another time they asked: "Is it *lawful* to give
tribute to Caesar, or not?" (Mark 12:14). In each

case it was a question of Jewish law. So also in the exchange between Jesus and the Pharisees when they inquired: "Is it *lawful* for a man to put away his wife for every cause?" There was unity of definition on "lawful," "put away," "except," and "fornication."

Let's take the subject matter of this discussion point by point and see the logical order of thought from verse 3 to verse 9.

In verse 3, the Pharisees, with well-planned strategy, presented their test question about the legality of the Mosaic dissolution for every cause. As we have seen, this meant poor cooking, bad housekeeper, or if the Jew desired to marry a prettier girl, or any reason whatever.

In verses 4–6, Jesus went beyond the Deuteronomic law, which was the basis of the Pharisaic appeal, and took them back to the original law of marriage. Jesus, in reverting to the original, taught that the foundation of marriage was in the Creator's male-female-one-flesh purpose. The constitutional nature of man required a helpmeet of like nature. One was the completeness of the other.

"From the beginning it was not so." The Roman Catholic and Anglican theologians have argued at great length from these words to support their divorce-but-no-remarriage doctrine. All their teaching can be summed up in three points:

1. Jesus, in pointing to the original institution of marriage, showed the matrimonial union to be indissoluble.
2. Remarriage of the innocent party, while the guilty party is alive, is morally wrong.
3. Only death can sever the matrimonial bond.

We have disproved these arguments by showing

that the Mosaic divorce dissolved the union and allowed the woman to go and be another man's wife.

Jesus, in reverting to the original, gave affirmation
to the Creator's intent and purpose of marriage. The
divine ideal of the New Testament law has its basis
in the original. But in pointing to the first marriage,
Jesus showed us the perfection of Eden. Adam was not
an adulterer, nor was Eve an adulteress. There was
one man and one woman in the world.

In verses 4–6, divorce for adultery is not in view.
This does not enter the picture until verse 9.

Messiah ruled that what God hath "joined together," the Jews must not "put asunder." This *put
asunder* proves that Jesus spoke of divorce as being
dissolution. "Put asunder" means "to cut; split; break";
and the Deuteronomic divorce was a cutting of the
wedding bond, and Christ recognized it as such. Put
asunder certainly does not mean "separation from bed
and board."

There is a contrast between "joined together" and
"put asunder." The joined-together couple, when put
asunder, are no longer joined together.

It is true that from the beginning men did not
divorce their wives. But it is also true—as we shall
see later—that from the beginning men killed adulterous wives. No need to divorce them when they
killed them (Lev. 20:10).

In verse 7, the Jewish theologians used the main
thrust of their attack: Why did Moses allow a bill
of divorcement and to put her away? The Mosaic
precedent was dissolution with the right to remarriage
—and Jesus conceded the point. but said it was permitted for hardness of heart.

Jesus never said anything against the Mosaic death
penalty for adultery. And the death enactments were

still on the Jewish statute books. Jesus admitted this, and also referred to it (Matt. 15:4; John 8:3-7). See also John 19:7.

We may note in passing that, from the beginning, neither was there a separation from bed and board.

In verse 9, Jesus gave a one-sentence summation of the whole matter. Whoever put away—put asunder —his wife, except for fornication, and married another, committed adultery. The Pharisees had Jesus' answer to *their* question, as presented by them—and as understood by them.

In verses 3-9, the legal term "put away" was used four times in this discussion—twice by the Pharisees and twice by Jesus. Three times, in verses 3, 7, 8, on both sides, this term meant dissolution. Then by what word-magic does it become "separation" in verse 9? Jesus didn't use double talk. The meaning was not shifting back and forth from dissolution to separation.

Professor John H. Wigmore, the legal authority, warned us about interpreters who make words mean what they want them to mean. He called them "word magicians." He said they come to a word they want to change and say "Presto! Change." And that is what many people do with this subject in Matthew 19.

They come to verse 9, and without the least indication from Christ, then Presto! and a legal term with 14 centuries of dissolution usage suddenly and mysteriously becomes separation from bed and board. What is the result when this is done with other Bible words? The result is Christian Science, Unitarianism, and all the other *isms* that destroy the meaning of God's Word.

The separation-interpreters "ignore and defy the context, and bring in a strange and foreign thought" to this passage. Dissolution lies deep in this context, and "the context is the final court of appeal" (*A Manual*

Grammar of the Greek New Testament, Dana & Mantey, p. 259, 25th edition, Macmillan). To try to fit "separation" into this passage would be like trying to open a lock with the wrong key.

Both sides were discussing marriage as dissolved by divorce, and not as dissolved by death.

> A fundamental principle in grammatical-historical exposition is that words and sentences can have but one signification in one and the same connection. The moment we neglect this principle we drift out upon a sea of uncertainty and conjecture. (*Biblical Hermeneutics,* p. 103, Terry, M. S., 1895.)

The last part of verse 8 is a major argument of our opponents: "... from the beginning it was not so." But immediately after these words, Jesus added: "Whosoever shall put away his wife, except it be for fornication. ..." So, in verse 9, Jesus allowed a divorce. which, in verse 8, He said was not so from the beginning.

Why then did He allow a divorce when it was not so from the beginning?

Why didn't He say, "It was not so from the beginning, and it shall not be so now"?

There is only one reasonable answer. Fornication was an exception to all that Jesus taught about marriage and divorce. What we learned about "except" comes into play again. We could go through a complicated grammatical argument about the exception applying to both clauses, but it isn't necessary. It is sufficient, as we have proved, that the exception signifies "to exclude from the scope of statement or enactment"—"to exclude from an aggregate under consideration." Like this:

1. The original male-female purpose in marriage remains in force, except for fornication.
2. The man must forsake father and mother and cleave unto his wife, except for fornication.
3. What God hath joined together, man must not put asunder, except for fornication.
4. It was hardness of heart for a Jew to divorce his wife, except for fornication.
5. A Jew must not use the writing of divorcement, except for fornication.

It is a conclusion of fact that the Christ-authorized divorce of verse 9 made void the status of the woman as the man's wife. Separation from bed and board was not the subject-matter of the discussion.

Marriage can be made null and void for a violation of the one-flesh purpose. It can be dissolved for a violation of the thing that constitutes it. The *Pulpit Commentary*, long held in high honor, says: "Our Lord does not say that the remarriage of divorced persons is in all cases adulterous" (V. 36, p. 67, old edition).

In our parallel columns of Matthew and Mark we saw that Mark gives the general law of marriage and Matthew gives the exception to it. There is no contradiction between the two Gospels.

> The conclusion is, therefore, that there is no contradiction, and that Matthew 19:9 accords to the innocent spouse the right to remarriage. (*Baker's Dictionary of Theology*, p. 176, Baker Book House, 1960.)

Martin Luther held the same view, and in his sermon on marriage at Wittenberg in 1525 he said that "Matthew 19:9 is a blunt, clear, plain text. . . ."

Dr. G. Campbell Morgan, long esteemed "the greatest Bible expositor of the past century," held that marriage could be dissolved for the cause of sexual sin. He wrote that marriage is "indissoluble . . . save for the one, and only sin" (*The Gospel According to Matthew,* p. 238, Fleming Revell Co., 1929).

(The reader may ponder an interesting sidelight on this divorce question in verses 10–12. When Jesus handed down His new divorce law, the apostles thought it was so strict that it made it better for a man not to marry, but Jesus corrected their misconception and told them about the eunuchs.)

8

Are Fornication Exceptions Genuine?

We must now deal with the challenge that the Matthaean fornication exceptions are forgeries. Some claim that the words "except it be for fornication" were not in the ancient manuscripts and are not authentic. The importance of the exceptions is indicated by the many learned attempts for their excision.

If all the Scriptures that critics have claimed are fraudulent were cut out of the Bible, all that would be left would be the *Mutilated Version*. Not only texts and whole passages have been challenged as spurious, but every book in the New Testament has been challenged by someone.

The exceptions have strong authoritative support for their rightful places in both the texts found in Matthew 5:32 and 19:9. They have been accepted as genuine by the great body of New Testament scholars for 19 centuries. The leading church fathers, both Eastern and Western, accepted them. A long list of critical commentaries, encyclopedias, and translators have received them. The King James revisers and all the revision committees since 1611 have accepted them. The Westcott-Hort text has them. The Nestle text has them.

Some of the ablest and most quoted scholars who deny the authenticity of the exceptions have admitted that if the exceptions are genuine, they allow the right to remarriage after divorce for adultery. Bishop Charles

Gore of London was one of the foremost of these men.
In his oft-quoted book *The Question of Divorce*, Charles
Gore, D.D., D.C.L., LL.D., pp. 19–20 (1911), he
stated—*but gave no proof*—that the exceptions are not
genuine. He admitted that the exceptions, if genuine,
apply to remarriage as well as to divorce. He said the
exception in Matthew 19:9—

> ". . . leaves no doubt that divorce is used in such
> a sense as covers permission to remarry."

The learned bishop was wise enough to see this,
but he deluded himself with deceptive reasoning in his
scholastic attempts to deny the authenticity of the
exceptions.

The Roman Catholic theologians admit the exceptions have caused them much difficulty, but they
concede their authenticity. They wrote in their international work of reference:

> Some have tried to answer the difficulty by cast-
> ing doubt on the authenticity of the entire phrase
> of Matt. 19:9, (except it be for fornication),
> but the words are in general fully vouched for
> by the most reliable codices [manuscripts].
> (*Catholic Encyclopedia*, V. 5, p. 56, 1913.)

Those who say the exceptions are fraudulent can
do much for their cause if they can disprove this Roman
Catholic statement—"*fully vouched for by the most
reliable codices.*" If they cannot refute it, then it is
strong and convincing evidence against them.

Here's further proof from the *International Standard Bible Encyclopedia* (V. 2, p. 865, 1952):

> This may be said: Matthew's record stands in
> ancient MSS authority, Greek and also the
> Versions. And on this point let it be noted

that the testimony of the MSS was up before the English and American Revisers, and they have deliberately reaffirmed the text of 1611 and given us the exception in Christ's rule in each place, Mt. 5:32; 19:9. This makes the matter as nearly *res adjudicata* as can be done by human reason. ["res adjudicata" means "a question authoritatively and finally settled."]

We must realize that if the fornication exceptions are forgeries, then the original "one flesh" law of marriage becomes mandatory. The original law of marriage in Mark 10:3–9 and Luke 16:18 is absolute—no exception for anything, not even for separation from bed and board. In Mark and Luke there is no exception for adultery, incest, sodomy, harlotry, or any of the sex crimes.

The original law of marriage commands a man to "cleave to his wife; and they twain shall be one flesh." If there is no exception to this absolute law, then if a man's wife is a harlot, he must cleave to her. Those married to sex perverts must be one flesh with them, unless an exception can be found.

Hebrews 7:22; 8:6 says that Christ gave humanity a "better covenant" than the Mosaic Covenant; but Moses, with an inferior covenant, killed the adulterers and sex criminals and set the guiltless mates free to remarry. So, if the better covenant requires the guiltless to be one flesh with sex offenders, then it seems that Moses gave the guiltless a better deal.

If the exceptions are forgeries, would not the Divine Author of the New Testament have prevented such an error being put in His Word?

Many millions of copies of the New Testament have been distributed in our generation alone. So, if the exceptions are fraudulent, has not this been an enormous error for millions of Christians for 20 centuries?

Both Eastern and Western fathers accepted the Matthaean exceptions. The King James revisers and all the revision committees since 1611 have accepted them. The Westcott-Hort and Nestle texts have them. The Roman Catholic scholars say the exceptions are "fully vouched for by the most reliable codices." This is more than sufficient evidence to satisfy a reasonable mind.

9

Why Matthew Records
Fornication Exceptions

Matthew recorded the fornication exception twice. Mark and Luke do not record it. Some no-remarriage teachers have made a big argument about this apparent contradiction, but these same teachers are not disturbed about the differences in the Gospel records on other subjects, and they are important ones.

Modern critics have never ceased their attack on the Bible about its supposed contradictions, and many Bible scholars have written numerous books to defend it against this charge. Why then are there apparent discrepancies in the Gospels on divorce and other important subjects? Why did one Gospel writer report details that the others did not? Why did Matthew alone report the exceptions in the divorce law? Let's ask the most qualified scholars.

> And should we not learn ... that what appear to us strange omissions, which, when held by the side of the other Gospel narratives, seem to involve discrepancies, may be capable of the most satisfactory explanation, if we only knew all the circumstances?

> The accounts of the three Synoptic Gospels must be carefully pieced together. It will be seen that only thus can they be understood ... St. Mark, who gives only a very condensed ac-

count, omits this clause (except it be for fornication); but in Jewish circles the whole controversy between different teachers turned upon
this point. All held that divorce was lawful,
the only question being as to its grounds. (*The
Life and Times of Jesus the Messiah,* Edersheim,
Alfred, V. 2, p. 647; V. 1, p. 472; V. 2,
p. 332, Eerdmans Pub. Co., 1953.)

Dean Alford, eminent New Testament scholar,
said that in the Gospels there are "unaccountable varia-
tions" and "startling discrepancy for which no solu-
tions have been found" (*The Greek New Testament
for English Readers,* pp. 313, 321, 343, Moody Press).

Calvin said, "God gave us four Gospels that we
might have four views." ... "Certainly, the Divine
Author was not at variance with Himself." If each
Gospel had all the details of the others, what would be
the need for the four of them? The *Pulpit Commentary*
has some valuable information on *contradictions, omis-
sions, and discrepancies* in the Gospels.

> Each of the Evangelists records some words and
> actions of our Lord which are peculiar to him-
> self. ... Matthew alone preserves whole groups
> of special instructions and events. ... One Gospel
> would be perplexing and baffling without the
> facts and testimonies of the other Gospels.

> (There are) striking discrepancies and difficult
> omissions for which there is no explanation. ...
> The paragraphs ... containing matter peculiar to
> Matthew are not fewer than 62. (*Pulpit Com-
> mentary,* John, xcvi-xcvii, old edition.)

> The plain reconciliation of the passages (on
> divorce) must be found in the principle that

an exception in a fuller account must explain a
briefer one. . . . Mark and Luke might naturally
take this for granted without expressing it.
(*McClintock-Strong Encyclopedia*, V. 2, p. 841,
1878.)

The Scripture doctrine of divorce is very simple.
It is contained in Matt. 19:3–12. . . . In Matthew
we have the fullest report, containing everything that is reported elsewhere and one or two
important observations that the other writers
have not included. . . . Luke has but one verse
where Matthew has ten. Luke's verse is in no
necessary connection with the context. . . . We
seem to be justified then in saying that the total
doctrine of the Scripture pertaining to divorce
is contained in Matt. 19. . . . There is the issue
stated so plainly that the 'wayfaring man need
not err therein.' (*International Standard Bible
Encyclopedia*, V. 2, p. 865, Eerdmans, 1952.)

Matthew, Mark, and Luke must be studied together. If not, there will be seeming contradictions on
many subjects. These three Gospels are called the Synoptic Gospels. The word synoptic (*syn*, together, plus
opsis, view) means "to view together." Dean Alford
said:

It should be a maxim for every expositor and
every student, that Scripture is a *whole*, and
stands or falls together. (*The New Testament
for English Readers*, p. 29.)

Legal experts agree with biblical authorities on the
rule of unity. If you were involved in a legal case
about a transaction that had been negotiated with
various writings or documents, the court would use

this rule to arrive at a fair interpretation. Here is a quote from a British authority who is studied in American law schools:

> Every part (must be) collected and brought into action.... (We must) collect from the whole one uniform and consistent sense. (*Principles of Legal Interpretation*, Broom, Herbert, p. 29, London, 1937.)

> To interpret and reconcile laws so that they harmonize is the best code of construction. (*Corpus Juris Secundum*, V. 48, p. 112, American Law Book Co., 1947.)

When we wish to learn what Christ taught on any subject we must not confine ourselves to one Gospel but must look at the other Gospels for other details they may have. Only thus will a subject stand in harmony. This is true of many subjects in the Gospels. Examples: Matthew's account of the Sermon on the Mount has 111 verses, and Luke's has 29. Would not much be lacking if we had only Luke's record?

Matthew's account of the Olivet Discourse has 97 verses, and Mark's has 37. What could we do without Matthew's record of our Lord's great prophetic discourse? Why then do our opposing friends prefer Mark's "condensed account" of divorce when they prefer Matthew's "fuller account" of other subjects?

If the reasonings of some interpreters about Gospel differences hold good, then by the same reasoning we can argue that there were "four different crucifixions and four different resurrections" (Alford). The Bible would be an unreliable witness to the world if it contained contradictions.

Many New Testament authorities agree that Matthew has highest rank in the Gospel records.

"While Matthew fully records the discourses of our Lord . . . Mark reproduces (them) in a condensed form. . . . One Gospel completes the other" (Vincent). "Matthew most fully reports the words . . . " (Edersheim). There are "whole blocks of material which are peculiar" to Matthew (*Revelation and the Bible*, p. 244, Editor, Carl F. H. Henry).

One clear statement in God's Word is sufficient to settle any question. Jesus proved the resurrection of the dead to the Sadducees by an *inference from a single text* (Matt. 22:32).

Biblical authorities on interpretation tell us to follow the scientist and use his methods of interpretation, and scientists say:

> One exception disproves a hypothesis with just as much scientific certainty as a thousand.

Simon Greenleaf, professor of law at Harvard University (1833–48), was one of the top legal authorities of his day. He was also an expert in the Scriptures and wrote a valuable book on the Gospels in which he dealt with the subject of discrepancies.

> The discrepancies between the narratives of the several Evangelists, when carefully examined, will not be found sufficient to invalidate their testimony. Many seeming contradictions will prove, upon closer scrutiny, to be in substantial agreement.

> If the evidence of the Evangelists is to be rejected because of a few discrepancies among them, we shall be obliged to discard that of many of the contemporaneous histories on which we are accustomed to rely.

> Every document, apparently ancient . . . and

> bearing on its face no evident marks of forgery,
> the law presumes to be genuine, and devolves on
> the opposing party the burden of proving it to be
> otherwise. (*Testimony of the Evangelists Examined by Evidence Administered in Courts of Law*,
> pp. 33–34, 1874.)

Any argument against the exceptions in Matthew backfires, because, if discrepancy invalidates Matthew's exceptions, what becomes of their "separation from bed and board"? They have no place to turn for an exception but to Matthew.

But, some argue: "How can five words (except it be for fornication) change all that Jesus taught about marriage and allow a dissolution?" And we reply: In the same way that five words can change all that He taught about marriage and allow a separation.

Five words can modify a thousand words—or ten thousand. They can, and do, modify whole paragraphs or entire sections of a law or document.

I have referred to Mr. Elmer Miller, a lawyer who knows his Bible. He answered this objection by pointing out that God put some of His laws in four or five words:

Thou shalt not kill.

Thou shalt not steal.

Thou shalt not covet.

Thou shalt not commit adultery.

This is sufficient answer to those who call us the "Five-Word School."

We conclude that each of the Gospels contains important information the other does not have. Matthew has many details that Mark and Luke do not have. And Mark and Luke have many points that Matthew does not record.

If Matthew's account is rejected on details that he

alone records, must we not likewise reject details that Mark and Luke alone record?

Matthew provides us with the information respecting two additional reservations made by our Lord in this connection, that a man may put away his wife, and when he does he may marry another. (*Baker's Dictionary of Theology*, p. 170, 1960.)

10

The Meaning of Romans 7:1–4

1. Know ye not brethren, (for I speak to them that know the law,) how that the law hath dominion over a man as long as he liveth?

2. For the woman which hath a husband is bound by the law to her husband as long as he liveth; but if the husband be dead, she is loosed from the law of her husband.

3. So then if, while her husband liveth, she be married to another man, she shall be called an adulterous: but if her husband be dead, she is free from that law; so that she is no adulteress, though she be married to another man.

4. Wherefore, my brethren, ye also are become dead to the law by the body of Christ, that ye should be married to another.

Opposing writers come to these verses and repeat their arguments that only death can dissolve marriage. We must follow them and apply similar rules and arguments as we did in previous chapters, and we shall see that these verses do not teach that only death can dissolve the marriage bond.

Divorce for adultery is not in view in this Scripture. It states the general law of marriage, but it is modified by Matthew's exception for adultery. Mark and Luke also stated the general law but we have seen that it was modified by Matthew's exception.

We shall see in the next chapter that I Corinthians 7:15 is an exception to Romans 7:2. We appeal again to the *rule of unity*. We shall see that in the divorce cases of I Corinthians 7:15, Paul said: "A brother or sister is not under bondage in *such cases*."

The general law here says that a woman is in bondage to her husband. But when Paul wrote about the "such cases" in I Corinthians 7:15, he said a woman was *not* under bondage to her husband. These cases were exceptions to the general law of marriage.

In verses 1–4, Paul used an illustration from marriage to show that any power or authority that has been canceled is made void. We are "dead to the law by the body of Christ," that we should be "married to another."

In the 6th chapter, Paul had presented his doctrine that the death of Christ gives us deliverance from the Law and that we are free from it. The subject of chapter 6 is continued in chapter 7, and in the progress of his argument an illustration was needed. The general law of marriage was useful to this purpose.

Professor John Murray of Westminster Seminary, Philadelphia, wrote that Paul's allusion to the law of marriage was "incidental to Paul's main purpose," and:

> We must not fall into the mistake of loading his illustration with more significance than reasonably belongs to it in the context. (*Divorce*, p. 79, 1953.)

Paul said a woman is free from the "law of her husband" at his death. The husband, by right of marriage law, ruled over his wife by the power invested in him. She was in subjection to his marital authority. The husband's death released the woman from her husband's power over her and the legal connection was broken. The dominion of a law ceased when the one who exercised the law died. It is fundamental with Paul that "where no law is, there is no transgression" (Rom. 4:15). When a marriage is dissolved for adultery, the "law" of the husband no longer exists.

Paul, in verse 1, said he spoke to them that knew the law, both Jewish and Roman law. They knew the law of marriage, and they knew the Deuteronomic divorce law that "loosed" a woman from the law of her husband, and loosed it so completely that she "could go and be another man's wife," and she was not called an adulteress in the second marriage, nor in the third marriage if divorced in the second.

All Israel honored the writing of divorcement. No one dared to call the divorced woman an adulteress if she remarried while her first husband lived.

The Judaic law revoked the law of her husband. So also does the law of Christ in Matthew 5:32; 19:9. Whether dissolved by Moses, Christ, or death, the nature and effect of the dissolution is the same. All three released the woman from the law.

> The Jews have it that a woman 'is loosed from the law of her husband' by only one of two things: death or a letter of divorce; hence Romans 7:2–3. (*Sketches of Jewish Social Life*, Edersheim, Alfred, p. 158, Eerdmans, 1957.)

The marriage law in Romans is absolute. Death is the only exception to it. This law, unmodified, binds a wife to an adulterous husband for life. It has no provision for a separation from bed and board.

The "law of her husband" does not allow a separation; it forbids it. Isn't it contrary to this law to give a wife a *separation* from what she is *bound* to? If there is no exception to this law, is not a wife bound to a sex criminal or adulterer "as long as he liveth"?

As Romans was written about 25 years after Christ legislated on divorce in Matthew 5:32; 19:9, it is necessary that we understand Paul by Christ.

Archbishop R. C. Trench wrote:

> ... another rule of interpretation, as of common sense, which is, that we are not to expect in *every place* the whole circle of Christian truth, and that nothing is proved by the absence of a doctrine from one passage, which is clearly stated in others.

> (Some) came not to the Scripture to ... learn its language but to see if they could compel it to speak theirs, with no desire to draw *out of* Scripture its meaning, but only to thrust into Scripture their own [his emphasis]. (*Notes on the Parables*, p. 41, 1890.)

What the Law of Marriage Was From the Beginning

Paul said the Romans knew both civil and divine law. They knew that the law of God and man had put severe penalties upon adultery from the Genesis period. A few facts from biblical history show that unfaithfulness to the wedding covenant was always a major offense in the family life of the nation, and that God and man judged it with the same degree of condemnation. We note five points.

1. Genesis 38:24. During pre-Mosaic times, adulterous wives were put to death. Judah, not knowing that he had been trapped in his own sin, commanded of adulterous Tamar: "Bring her forth, and let her be burnt." Jewish history shows the Hebrew father and husband as the absolute master of his household, and that he had the undisputed power, before Moses, to

order the death of any female in his family who was
guilty of adultery.

2. Job 31:9–11. Old Testament authorities agree that
Job is one of the oldest books in the Bible. Job here
said that adultery "is an heinous crime; yes, it is an
iniquity to be punished by the judges."

3. Numbers 5:12–31. When a Jew suspected his
wife of adultery, but had no proof, he could bring her
to the priest who made her drink water mixed with
dust from the Tabernacle floor. She was put under
an oath:

> If thou hast gone aside to another instead of thy
> husband, and if thou be defiled, and some man
> have lain with thee beside thy husband . . . the
> Lord make thee a curse. . . . And this water that
> causeth the curse shall go into thy bowels, to
> make thy belly to swell, and thy thigh to rot;
> and the woman shall say, Amen, Amen. Then
> shall the man be *guiltless* from iniquity, and
> this woman shall bear her iniquity. (Numbers
> 5:20–22, 31.)

The husband was "guiltless" in bringing his adulterous wife to the priest that the curse of God might
come upon her. His action was not caused by hardness
of heart. God did not require a Jew to "cleave to" and
be "one flesh" with an adulterous wife whose body
swelled and rotted under His curse. He could divorce
her and remarry and be guiltless while she still lived
in her God-cursed body.

4. Leviticus 20:10; Deuteronomy 22:22. "The
adulterer and the adulteress shall surely be put to
death." "So shalt thou put away evil from Israel."

Adultery in the Hebrew State was unforgivable
and deadly. The guiltless could not forgive the guilty

and have them spared. Execution was mandatory. It was a "sin unto death." "He that despised Moses law died without mercy under two or three witnesses" (Heb. 10:28). Divorce would have been merciful.

"Put away evil from Israel." Adultery was looked upon with such abhorrence that it was put in the category of capital crimes. It was a crime against the Hebrew State, and also against the divine law. Governmental condemnation of adultery did not mean personal revenge or hardness of heart. It was a crime against the moral interests of the Israelic community. Man's relation to the moral universe requires his obedience to moral laws.

Punishment of adultery was a moral necessity. It was also a preventive measure. Innocent mates are often infected with venereal disease by an adulterous partner. Babies are born blind and afflicted. Harlot mothers make harlot daughters, and adulterous fathers are a bad influence on their sons. Such social perils were to be avoided in the State of Israel. The sexual abominations of surrounding heathen nations could not go unpunished in the Jewish nation.

Moses punished the guilty and set the innocent free to remarry. He did not bind virtue with the chains of debauchery. And in the New Testament law of divorce and remarriage, one stroke of the divine sword sets the forgiving party free from the one who refuses all attempts toward reconciliation. Christ did not abolish the right to "put away evil" in an adulterous marriage.

The Romans knew that ancient civilizations punished adultery by cutting off the nose and ears of the person unfaithful to the conjugal covenant. Such bodily mutilation was inflicted by the Chaldeans and Egyptians (*Diod.* Sic. 1. 89–90). God threatened harlot Israel with this punishment. He said that in His "jealousy" He would send Israel's enemies against her and "they shall take away thy nose and thine ears; and thy remnant shall fall by the sword" (Ezek. 23: 19–25).

> Adultery, therefore, if fully ascertained, must be punished with death, as a practice subversive of the whole design of the theocratic constitution. (*The Typology of Scripture*, Fairbairn, Patrick, 2. 349, Zondervan.)

5. Paul, in I Corinthians 5:9–11, told the Corinthian church "not to company with fornicators," and, "with such an one not to eat." And in verse 5, a fornicator was to be delivered "unto Satan for the destruction of the flesh. . . ."

Paul gave "vehement emphasis" to the offense of the Corinthian fornicator and demanded his expulsion on the ground of the Deuteronomic Law (*Expositors Greek Testament*, V. 2, p. 813). As God banished fornicators from fellowship with His church, would He require His saints to be "one flesh" with them?

Divorce for adultery was compulsory among ancient Jews. And in ancient Athens a citizen was deprived of civil rights if he refused to divorce an adulterous wife. Paul referred to the practice of shaving the head of an adulteress and driving her from home (I Cor. 11:6).

During Cromwell's ascendancy in England, adultery was punishable by death. In countries where Jews held positions of political power, adultery was punished by flagellation and imprisonment. In America, for centuries it has frequently happened that a husband or wife has killed an adulterous mate, then pled the "unwritten law," and twelve fellow citizens acquitted them—set them free to be married to another.

Yes, the Romans knew the law. They knew the Roman law which is the basis of all modern law. They knew the Deuteronomic law allowed the divorced woman to be another man's wife without being called an adulteress.

They knew the law codes of ancient nations that inflicted severe penalties for adultery. The famous Hammurabi Code (2000 B.C.) inflicted death upon an adulteress by drowning. The Babylonian and Assyrian codes before Hammurabi were likewise severe. There were striking similarities of punishments for crimes in the Deuteronomic code and the codes of other nations. (See *Israel's Laws and Legal Precedents*, Kent, C. F., Charles Scribner's & Sons, 1907.)

The no-remarriage expositors put much reliance for their doctrine on these verses in Romans 7. It is a stronghold for their teaching that only death can dissolve the marital bond. But the evidence is decisive for the conclusion that divorce and remarriage for adultery was not within the scope of Paul's thought in these verses.

11

The Meaning of First Corinthians 7:10–15

10. And unto the married I command, yet not I, but the Lord, Let not the wife depart from her husband:

11. But and if she depart, let her remain unmarried, or be reconciled to her husband: and let not the husband put away his wife.

Some teachers argue from these verses that divorce does not dissolve marriage because the woman in the case of verse 11 was commanded to "remain unmarried."

The word "depart" in verses 10–11 signifies divorce. The standard Greek lexicons define "depart" (*chorizo*) as:

"a. to leave a husband or wife: of divorce. I. Cor. 7:11, 15." (*Thayer's Greek-English Lexicon of the New Testament*, p. 674.)

A Greek-English Lexicon of the New Testament, Arndt & Gingrich, p. 898.

Manual Greek Lexicon of the New Testament, Abbot-Smith, p. 486.

The New Testament in Greek, Westcott & Hort, Lexicon, p. 211, 1953.

Depart. (Chorizo), divorce. "Oft. in marriage contracts in the papyri . . . 1. Cor. 7:1, 11, 15." (Arndt & Gingrich, p. 898.)

The scriptural divorce separated in the sense that it "divided" the couple and dissolved the union. It is a major error to say that the scriptural divorce was a separation that left the marriage undissolved.

The woman in the case of verse 11 had obtained a divorce according to Greek law, which was easy to get, but Paul refused to recognize the validity of the divorce. The fact that the woman had obtained a divorce is indicated by his command for the woman to remain "unmarried." She was commanded to remain unmarried or be reconciled to her husband because the decree she obtained did not dissolve the marriage. She was still the wife of the man she divorced. The divorce had left the marriage undissolved as in the case of Matthew 5:32. If she had divorced her husband for adultery, the case would have been different.

A study of chapter 7 shows that a strong movement against married life had developed in Corinth. Some believed that the marital relations were impure, and that through abstinence they could attain to a higher spiritual state. This belief frequently appears in the Christian Church.

This ascetic belief has continued from the church fathers to our day. There was a "craze of celibacy" among some of the early Christians and church fathers. It was also among some of the mystical religious groups before Christ. It is a sad fact today that many believing the married sex relations to be sinful, have broken up their homes and have driven their mates into adultery.

The monks of the Western church had a strong aversion to marriage, and this spirit of celibacy influenced their interpretation of the divorce Scriptures, as well as profoundly affecting the civil divorce legislation of the countries where they held positions of power.

It is uncertain whether the woman in the case of verse 11 was a member of the Celibacy Party in Corinth, but whatever the reason for divorcing her husband, she did not have valid ground for the divorce.

It is a point of critical importance to note that when Jesus gave His divorce commandment in Matthew 5:32; 19:9, He did not specify this all-important point to "remain unmarried." If He had, then this divorce question would have been settled forever. *Why was the Lord careful to specify "remain unmarried" in one case of divorce but not in another?* Is it not because in one case He recognized marriage as dissolved by divorce but in the other case He did not?

Would the Lord have commanded the woman in the case of verse 11 to be reconciled to her husband if she had divorced him for adultery? Surely, Jesus would not give a woman the right to "put away" an adulterous husband and then command her to be "reconciled" to him.

If the wife in the case of verse 11 had divorced her husband—with the Greek dissolution-divorce—on the ground that he was a convicted sex-perverted criminal, would the Lord have commanded her to return to him? When we ask non-dissolution teachers these questions, they become vague—or silent.

In verse 11 the Lord also commanded: "Let not the husband put away his wife." (But he could put her away for fornication.) This commandment, unmodified, has no exception for anything. If the exception was not allowed, then the husband was bound by the from-the-beginning law to be one flesh with an adulteress.

The non-dissolution teachers have distorted the

meaning of verses 10–11. Leading conservative scholars agree that in verses 10–11, Paul was not dealing with divorce for adulterous marriage.

> Romanists have inferred from the text . . . and notwithstanding Matt. 5:32, that even adultery leaves the marriage vow binding on the wronged party, but this question is not in view here. (*Expositors Greek Testament*, V. 2, p. 826, Eerdmans, 1956.)

Those who quote verses 10–11 shy away from the exception in verse 15 where the apostle ruled on other cases of divorce, and said that those Christians who had been deserted and divorced were "not under bondage" to the married. The husband and wife in the case of verse 11 were under bondage to their marriage. Those in verse 15 were not. Why? What made the difference? We now consider this exception:

> But if the unbelieving depart, let him depart.
> A brother or sister is not under bondage in *such cases.*

Expositors are divided on the interpretation of this text. Some say it means the dissolution of marriage, but others deny this. Which side is right? Which side can *prove* it is right? The following proofs will defend our view for dissolution.

The whole question turns on the meaning of the words "not under bondage." Here again the importance of the *rule of definition* comes into play.

Verse 15 deals with a new problem that had developed in Corinth. When Corinthians became Christians, in some cases, the unbelieving husband or wife deserted and divorced the believer because of their faith in Christ. What should the Christians do in "such cases"? They wrote to Paul for his answer to this new problem, and he replied:

> 12. If any brother hath a wife that believeth not, and she be pleased to dwell with him, let him not put her away.
>
> 13. And the woman which hath a husband that believeth not, and if he be pleased to dwell with her, let her not leave him. . . .
>
> 15. But if the unbelieving depart, let him depart. A brother or sister is not under bondage in such cases: but God hath called us to peace.

Opponents have argued that if *not under bondage* signifies the dissolution of marriage, it would be a contradiction of Matthew 5:32; 19:9, where the only ground for dissolution is fornication. Many outstanding scholars say there is no contradiction. Dr. C. I. Scofield wrote:

> So far from disclaiming inspiration, the apostle associates his teaching with the Lord's. Cases had arisen (e.g. 12–16) as the Gospel overflowed Jewish limitations, not comprehended in the words of Jesus (Mt. 5:31; 19:5–9), which were an instruction primarily to Israel. These new conditions demanded authoritative settlement, and only the inspired words of an apostle could give that. (*The Scofield Bible*, I Cor. 7:15, Oxford University Press.)

The Greek word for "depart" (*chorizo*) in verse 15 signifies divorce as in verse 11. Four leading Greek lexicons were previously cited as proof for this.

When the New Testament was written in Greek

and sent to the cities of the Empire, the "writing of
divorcement" (*biblion apostasion*) was universally
understood as signifying dissolution. This was also a
term used in business transactions, official and legal
documents.

Greek was the most exact language in the world,
and the Holy Spirit selected this language for the writing of the New Testament (even if some parts of it
were originally written in Aramaic).

To show the kind of divorce the unbelievers obtained when they divorced the Christians, we now see
the testimony of the highest New Testament authorities.

> Bill of Divorcement (*Apostasion*).
> "apostasion, a legal term, found as early as
> Lysias, Hyperid . . . and Demosth., and frequent-
> ly in papyri . . . in the sense of relinquishment of
> property after sale, abandonment, etc. The con-
> sequent giving up of one's claim explains the
> meaning which the word acquires in Jewish cir-
> cles . . . (Jer. 3:8) give (one's wife) a certificate
> of divorce. Mt. 19:7 . . . with the same meaning
> in Matt. 5:31." (*A Greek-English Lexicon of
> the New Testament and Early Christian Litera-
> ture*, Arndt & Gingrich, p. 97, University of
> Chicago Press, 1957.)

Greek scholars refer to Moulton & Milligan's *Vocabulary of the Greek New Testament* as the "final
court of appeals" on New Testament usage because it
gives illustrations of New Testament words from the
papyri and other non-literary sources. This is what
they have on "Bill of Divorcement":

> *Apostasion*—bond of relinquishing . . . a contract
> of renunciation . . . the renunciation of rights of

ownership ... a deed of divorce. (page 69.)

Our evidence proves that the divorce obtained by the unbeliever was a renunciation of the marriage and a forfeiture of all marital claims. And *the Lord recognized the Greek divorce as having dissolved the marriage.*

Westermarck, the *Encyclopaedia Britannica* authority on marriage, wrote in his *Short History of Marriage*, p. 286 (Macmillan Co.):

> Among the Greeks of the Homeric Age divorce seems to have been almost unknown, but afterward it became an every day event in Greece. According to the Attic law, the husband could repudiate his wife whenever he liked and without stating any motives, but he was compelled to send his divorced wife back to her father's house with her dowry. The wife could demand a divorce by applying to the Archon and stating the motives for her demand.

In I Corinthians 7:10–11, the reference is to a married couple, *both of whom are believers*. But 7:15 refers to a marriage where one was a believer and the other an unbeliever, and where the believer does not put away—but is put away.

In this case of 7:15, the Christian did not divorce the unbeliever, but the unbeliever divorced the believer. In the case of verses 10–11, the Lord did not recognize the divorce as having dissolved the marriage, but in the case of verse 15, He did. Is not this significant?

Let it also be noted that the word "depart" (chorizo) means to "put asunder." It is the same word that Jesus used in Matthew 19:6, when He said, "Let not man put asunder" (chorizo). Although the Lord said in

Matthew, "let not man put asunder," He accepted the Greek divorce as a valid dissolution when the heathen divorced the believer in the cases of I Corinthians 7:15.

(An interesting sidelight is that, under Moses, Jewish family members who tried to turn other family members to idolatry, were stoned to death, Deut. 18:6–10. And Dr. Edersheim wrote: "One of the cases in which divorce was obligatory was, if either party had become heretical, or ceased to profess Judaism."
—*Sketches of Jewish Life*, p. 158.)

We now turn our attention to the term "not under bondage" in verse 15. The key that unlocks the problem is the original definition of "bondage" (*douloo*). This word signified "slavery."

> "to make a slave of" ... "held by the constraint of law or necessity in some matter, I. Cor. 7:15." "Make someone a slave" ... "Be bound (as a slave) I. Cor. 7:15," "to enslave, bring into bondage."
>
> *Thayer's Greek-English Lexicon of the New Testament*, p. 158.
>
> *A Greek-English Lexicon of the New Testament*, Arndt & Gingrich, p. 205.
>
> *Manual Greek Lexicon of the New Testament*, Abbot-Smith, p. 122.
>
> *Expository Dictionary of New Testament Words*, Vine, W. E., V. 1, p. 139.
>
> *The New Testament in Greek*, Westcott & Hort, Lexicon, p. 49, 1953.

"If the unbelieving depart, let him depart. A brother or sister is not in bondage in such cases: but God

hath called us to peace." This means, in substance
and effect, that if the unbelieving mate obtained a
divorce, let him—or her—have it. The believer was
not to contest the divorce action by any wrangling or
legal maneuver to prevent it. God hath called us to
peace. Bitterness or strife was to be avoided.

The only way the believer could prevent the divorce was to deny the Lord Jesus Christ. This is true
in heathen countries today. It is true in America in
our time. Many Christians are faced with the same
problem. They must decide between Christ and the
unbelieving mate. Jews and Moslems are divorced by
their mates when they become Christians.

When an unbeliever obtained a divorce for this
reason, what was the marital status of the believer?
Must the believer "keep the door open" for the unbeliever to return at any time from the sex orgies of
vice-ridden Corinth, to resume the "one flesh" relation with the believer? Paul answered with an em-
phatic and decisive NO. The marriage was dissolved
—both by civil and New Testament law. The believer
was no longer a *slave* to the marriage. He, or she,
was *free* to remarry. If they could not remarry, they
certainly were in bondage, were they not?

What was it that the divorced Christians were not
in bondage to? By all the rules, there can be only one
answer: they were no longer in bondage to the marriage. Before the divorce they were in bondage—to
the marriage. After the divorce they were not in bondage—to the marriage. If, after the divorce, they were
still in bondage, *what* were they in bondage to?

Paul, in Romans 7:2, said the wife was "*bound
by the law to her husband so long as he liveth*," but
in the Corinthian case the same apostle said she was
not. Was Paul at variance with himself? Surely not.

Why was the command "remain unmarried" specified in the divorce case of verses 10–11, but not in the case of verse 15? Why didn't the Lord specify *remain unmarried* in Matthew 5:32; 19:9? Four times, when the Lord dealt with divorce (Matt. 5:32; 19:9; I Cor. 7:10–11; 7:15), He specified "remain unmarried" in *one* case but not in the other *three*. Why such a sharp distinction in *one* case?

"Under bondage" and "not under bondage" were legal terms used in the slave trade. The reader can see from the citations I gave that these terms had long established usage in business and legal matters.

When a slave master bought a slave, the slave was under the yoke of continuous service to his owner. Paul sent Onesimus back to Philemon his owner because he recognized the slave's bondage to him. But when Philemon gave Onesimus his freedom, as Paul suggested he would do, Onesimus would then be *free*. Philemon would then have no further claim on him. Onesimus was as free as the slaves that Lincoln liberated.

If a slave ran away, his owner could have him arrested and brought back. But if the slave had been legally declared "not under bondage," his former owner had no claim on him whatever. The slave's release was a "bond of relinquishing," "a contract of renunciation" (*apostasion*). This is exactly what the bill of divorcement did to the marriage in the case of I Corinthians 7:15.

High ranking New Testament authorities hold that *not under bondage* signifies the dissolution of marriage.

> Is not under bondage (*ou dedoulotai*). A strong word, indicating that Christianity has not made marriage a state of slavery to believers. Compare *dedetai is bound*, v. 39, a milder word. The

meaning clearly is that wilful desertion on the part of the unbelieving husband or wife sets the other party free. Such cases are not comprehended in Christ's words. (*Word Studies in the New Testament*, Vincent, M. R., V. 3, p. 219, Eerdmans, 1957.)

The Protestant commentators of the 16th and 17th centuries, or the large majority of them, draw the liberty of remarriage after desertion from the word of Paul, First Corinthians 7:15. [President Woolsey named some of these commentators and theologians, including Beza and Calixus.] (*Essay on Divorce and Divorce Legislation*, Theodore Woolsey, D.D., L.L.D., pp. 134–135, Scribner, 1869.)

I. Cor. 7:15. "She is not bound to remain unmarried and to wait for or to seek for reconciliation. (Grotius, Quoted by Woolsey, ibid., p. 135.)

Johann Neander (1789–1850), prominent German theologian and church historian, and professor of church history in Berlin from 1813, wrote:

Protestant exegesis has understood the apostle to the effect that in such a case, I. Cor. 7:15, the Christian party would be authorized to enter into a new marriage. (Quoted by Woolsey, ibid., p. 79.)

The Roman Catholic Church allows remarriage on the authority of I Corinthians 7:15. For their exceptions to indissoluble marriage, see Divorce, *Catholic Encyclopedia*, 1933.

Remarriage after divorce was allowed by church leaders in the earliest centuries of the church on the exceptions in Matthew 5:32; 19:9; I Corinthians 7:15. Origen, who lived in 185–254 A.D., is generally considered chief among the church fathers. He and Augustine are regarded the two greatest. Origen wrote that "Some bishops in his time permitted a woman to marry whilst her former husband was living" (*Hom. 7,* in Matt. 2. p. 67). (Quoted in *The Antiquities of the Christian Church,* Bingham, Joseph, V. 2, p. 1209, Reeves & Turner, London, 1878.)

This passage (7:15) is generally adduced as the Bible warrant for the view that wilful desertion is a sufficient reason for divorce. Such desertion is a *de facto* rupture of the marriage, and stands on the same footing as adultery. (*Pulpit Commentary,* V. 44, p. 251, old edition.)

I. Cor. 7:15, which allows remarriage where a Christian partner is deserted by a heathen. (*International Standard Bible Encyclopedia,* V. 3, p. 1999, Eerdmans Pub. Co., 1952. *Hastings Dictionary of the Bible,* p. 586, 1918.) ... if the unbeliever wishes to dissolve the union, it may be dissolved. (*The New Testament for English Readers,* Alford, Dean, p. 1014, Moody Press.)

I. Cor. 7:15. The Christian is not so enslaved by such an alliance that he or she may not be set free. (*Notes on the Epistles of Paul,* Bishop Lightfoot, p. 226.) The deserted party seems to be left more at liberty ... to marry another person. It does not seem reasonable that they should still be bound. ... In such a case marriage would be servitude indeed. (*Matthew Henry's Commentary,* 1st Cor. 7:15.)

A Companion to the Bible is a new reference work

by 36 scholars on the meanings of important Bible
words. It comments on I Corinthians 7:15:

> This divorce ... it would seem, authorizes a re-
> marriage, since the believer ceases to be bound
> (I Cor. 7:12–16); his previous marriage is now
> disqualified. (Oxford University Press, p. 257,
> 1958.)

The *Expositors Greek Testament,* a work by 17
Greek scholars, comments:

> The brother or sister in such circumstances is
> not kept in bondage; cf. v. 39.—the stronger
> verb of this passage implies that for the repudi-
> ated party to continue bound to the repudiator
> would be *slavery.* If ... the repudiator forms a
> new union, cutting off all hope of restoration,
> the case then appears to come under the excep-
> tion in Matt. 5:32.

> In such cases the Christian brother or sister is
> not tied to marriage. (*Moffatt's Translation.*)

> A brother or sister is not in the position of a
> slave ... in an indissoluble union in such cases
> as these. (*Wuest's Translation.* Eerdmans Pub.
> Co.)

Baker's Dictionary of Theology is a widely accepted work by 138 scholars from all over the world.
On page 28 we read:

> In verses 12 and 15, Paul addresses to Christians
> joined in mixed marriages to unbelievers a new
> provision, which Christ had not considered when
> addressing Jews, namely, that if the unbelieving
> spouse desires to break the marriage bond by de-
> serting the Christian, the latter is not bound,

but is free to marry. (Editor, Everett F. Harrison, Baker Book House, 1960.)

You may be interested to see the opinions of the following.

Martin Luther. 1. Cor. 7:15. "Here the Apostle rules that the unbeliever who deserts his wife should be divorced, and he pronounces the believer free to marry another." (*Reformation Writings of Martin Luther,* Woolf, B. L., p. 307, Lutterworth Press, London, 1952.)

Church Fathers. "The Fathers to some extent, and Catholics and Protestants, understood 7:15 to mean at liberty to contract a new marriage." (*McClintock & Strong Encyclopedia,* V. 2, p. 841, 1878.)

Many spiritually minded pastors believe that adultery or wilful and permanent desertion can kill a marriage as surely as though the guilty party were in his grave. (*Twentieth Century Encyclopedia of Religious Knowledge,* p. 344, Baker Book House, 1955.)

Here's one from the Archbishop of Canterbury that may surprise you. It surprised me.

I. Cor. 7:15. "But clearly St. Paul's direction is that a valid marriage may in these circumstances be ended, and a new marriage entered into." (*Problems of Divorce and Remarriage,* Dr. Geoffrey Fisher, p. 7. Morehouse & Gorham Co., N.Y., 1955.)

(Anglican opinion concerning the Matthaean exception has long been divided, shifting back and forth. The Lambeth Conference of 1888—

". . . noted that there had always been a difference of opinion in the Church on the question
whether our Lord meant to forbid marriage to
the innocent party."

The Lambeth Conference of 1908 resolved that it
was "undesirable that the innocent party should be
remarried with the blessing of the Church." This
position was won by the narrow margin of three votes
out of a total vote of 171. (See *Problems of Divorce
and Remarriage*, Dr. Geoffrey Fisher, p. 7.) The
Church of England will not marry a divorced person
but will give its blessing to the marriage if performed
by the minister of another denomination, and they will
admit the divorced and remarried persons into their
Church (See *Encyclopaedia Britannica*, V. 7, p. 514,
1965).)

Now, read verses 15 and 39 together. Use the *rule
of unity* on these verses. The general law of marriage
is stated in verse 39, as in Romans 7:2:

The wife is bound by the law as long as her
husband liveth; but if her husband be dead, she
is at liberty to be married to whom she will;
only in the Lord.

But in verse 15 the exception is given to this general law. So here we have the general law and the
exception to it in the same chapter. In the Gospels,
the general law was given in Mark and Luke but the
exception to it is twice stated in Matthew. So in
Matthew 5:32; 19:9; I Corinthians 7:15, there are
three exceptions to the general law. We have the required "two or three witnesses."

In the general law (v. 39), the wife is bound to
her husband for life. In the exception (v. 15), she is
not.

"Bondage" and "freedom" are strong words in Paul's vocabulary, and they stand in meaningful contrast in his epistles. When he used "not under bondage," he used one of the strongest terms in the most exact language in the world. Paul was learned in law and logic. "His writings show a wide knowledge of Greek and Roman laws and their institutions," and he must be "ranked as a great master of language." Why then did he use such a decisive legal term that signified the complete liberation of a slave from his master, and the total and final release from the bondage of matrimony?

Now let's see how verses 15, 27–28, 39 stand in contrast.

Art thou *bound* unto a wife? seek not to be *loosed*. Art thou loosed from a wife? seek not a wife. But and if thou marry, thou hast not sinned. . . (27–28).

Paul here spoke of being "loosed" from the bondage of marriage by divorce. "Art thou bound unto a wife? seek not to be loosed"—as some were doing without just cause in verses 10–11.

Much importance hangs on the meaning of "loosed." This word refers to divorce. The standard sources say:

Loosed, (*Lusis*), "A loosening. 1. Cor. 7:27, of divorce, is translated 'to be loosed,' lit., 'loosing.' " (*Expository Dictionary of New Testament Words*, Vine, W. E., V. 3, p. 16, 1940.)

Art thou bound to a wife? . . . Marriage bond as in Rom. 7:2.

Seek not to be loosed . . . "do not be seeking release" (*lusin*) from the marriage bond . . . (*Word Pictures in the New Testament*, Robertson, V. 4, p. 132, Broadman Press, 1931.)

Loosed, (*Lusis*) which in 1. Cor. 7:27 is used with reference to the "loosing" of the marriage tie, is common with reference to the "discharge" of bonds and debts. ... (*The Vocabulary of the Greek New Testament*, Moulton & Milligan, p. 382.)

So also:

The New Testament in Greek, Westcott & Hort, Lexicon, p. 114, 1953.

Manual Greek Lexicon of the New Testament, Abbott-Smith, p. 273. 1921.

A Greek Lexicon of the New Testament and Other Early Christian Literature, Arndt & Gingrich, p. 483, 1957.

A Patristic Greek Lexicon, Editor, G. W. H. Lampe, V. 3, p. 815.

A Greek Lexicon of the Roman and Byzantine Periods, Sophocles, E. A., p. 723, 1887.

Loosed, (*lusis*), (from Homer down), *a loosing of any bond*, as that of marriage; hence once in the New Testament of divorce. 1. Cor. 7:27. (*Thayer's Greek-English Lexicon*, p. 384.)

"Are you *bound* to a wife? Do not seek to be *free*. Are you *free* from a wife? Do not seek a wife." (*Amplified New Testament*, Zondervan.)

Why pile up all this evidence for one word? Because everything depends on its historical definition. *Bondage* expressed total enslavement. *Loosed* expressed total liberation.

Archbishop R. C. Trench wrote:

To study a people's language will be to study *them*, and to study them at best advantage.

Often a people's use of some single word will afford a deeper insight into their real condition, their habits of thought and feeling. than whole volumes written expressly with the intention of imparting this insight. (Suplee's *Trench on Words*, pp. 135–137.)

The apostle said to a man loosed from matrimonial bondage by biblical divorce: "But and *if thou marry, thou hast not sinned*" (v. 28).

Why did not Paul command this loosed-man to "remain unmarried"? Why did he not command him to "be reconciled" to his divorced wife? (*Lusis* is still used by Greeks for divorce and the cancellation of bonds and debts.)

Professor Robertson dedicated his *Word Pictures in the New Testament* to Dr. Adolf Deissmann of Berlin with the words, "Who has done so much to make the words of the New Testament glow with life." Students know about Deissmann's famous work, *Light From the Ancient East*. He gave us most of the proof we now possess about New Testament meanings. He insisted:

If we are ever in this matter to reach certainty at all, then it is the inscriptions and papyri which will give us the nearest approximation to the truth.

Until the papyri were discovered there were practically no other contemporary documents to illustrate that phase of the Greek language which comes before us in the LXX and NT.

(Quoted in *A Grammar of the Greek New Testa-*

ment in the Light of Historical Research, Robertson, A. T., p. 79, Broadman Press, 1934.)

Professor Deissmann (1866–1937) proved from the
papyri and inscriptions that the Apostle Paul used legal
language in his epistles. He wrote in his *Light From
The Ancient East* that:

> Paul had a "fondness for legal expressions . . . "
> and these expressions were "the language of
> the documents." (p. 119)

> Paul "was strongly influenced by legal ideas."
> (p. 318)

> Paul was "influenced by the popular law of the
> world in which he lived." (p. 320)

> On the subject of freedom from slavery, Paul
> "took his stand on this custom of the ancient
> world." (p. 327)

> The document of manumission for slaves con-
> tained the formula "free under earth and heav-
> en. . . " (p. 328)

> "The New Testament also uses technical terms
> of contemporary constitutional law . . . " (p.
> 342)

> Paul took terms "from the language of contem-
> porary constitutional law . . . " (p. 357)

Professor Deissmann said that anyone who does
not consider the history of Paul's words and meanings
is tearing Paul from his Greek world, and the Gospel
from history, and shutting off the New Testament from
the light of research (p. 407).

We conclude from this evidence that "not under
bondage" expressed the total release from the marital

bond, and that the Greek divorce bill *biblion apostasion* contained the same legal meaning of absolute dissolution as did the Jewish bill. *Biblion apostasion* is still in the law books of Greece.

If this evidence is not sufficient to convince a reasonable mind, then there is an end to all meaning in language and we must despair of ever proving anything.

To those who object that our interpretation of I Corinthians 7:15 adds an exception to Christ's law of divorce, we point out that some no-remarriage denominations allow an annulment of marriage for the cause of "fraud."

In civil law, the statute of frauds provides for the annulment of marriage with the right to remarriage. No-remarriage denominations accept this legal provision and grant an annulment of marriage with the right to remarriage, which makes our Lord's divorce law to mean, "except for fornication and fraud."

The reasoning behind the statute of frauds is that the hiding of a material fact, which one is morally bound to disclose before the marriage, justifies the annulment of marriage and allows remarriage. Such material fact is sexual impotence, sterility, epilepsy, insane tendencies, or any fact that was intended to deceive the marital partner.

The suppression of some fact or circumstance by silence or deception that causes injury or deprivation of rights to the marital partner, is sufficient ground for annulment. The pretense of normality where there is abnormality involves a breach of the conjugal covenant into which one is required to enter with good faith. Also, if the parties were intoxicated at the time of marriage, this is sufficient cause for annulment. (Some denominations, in granting annulments, require that the marriage must not have been sexually consummated.)

12

The Church Fathers' Views
On Divorce and Remarriage

Some non-dissolution interpreters say there is no evidence that any of the early church fathers believed that the New Testament law of divorce allowed remarriage. They claim that for the first 500 years of the Christian Church all the fathers were on their side of the divorce question. This is not true. But even if it were, a Bible doctrine is not to be decided by the fathers. The final authority is the Word of God.

Many of the church fathers believed that the three exceptive texts, Matthew 5:32; 19:9; I Corinthians 7: 15, permitted remarriage.

The *Dictionary of Christ and the Gospels* is a standard reference work. I quote:

At all periods of the history of Christian teaching, differences of opinion have existed within the Church as to the practical application of Jesus' words concerning adultery, divorce, and remarriage. These differences have been stereotyped in the Eastern and Western branches of the Catholic church. The former takes the more lenient view, and permits remarriage of the innocent.... [The latter denied it.]

On the other hand, the general consensus of theological opinion amongst English-speaking divines since the Reformation has leaned toward the view held by the Eastern church ... (V. 1, p. 31, Editor, James Hastings, 1906.)

A Companion to the Bible is a new reference work by 36 scholars. It says:

> ... the Eastern Church consistently saw in adultery a legitimate cause of divorce, which permits the remarriage of the divorcee, and *that at the Council of Trent the Church of Rome forebore to condemn the Eastern discipline on this point.* (Oxford Press, 1958. p. 257. my emphasis.)

Biblical scholars know the value of the *A Patristic Greek Lexicon*, which gives an abundance of references to show how biblical words were understood and used by the early church fathers. In this work we read: "Fornication (was) linked with adultery as ground for divorce, after which remarriage is allowable." (Oxford University Press, 1960, V. 4. p. 1121.)

On the question of remarriage after divorce for adultery, the *Jamieson, Fausset, Brown Commentary* comments:

> The Church of Rome says No; but the Greek and Protestant churches allow it. Matthew 5:32.

> The Oriental and most Reformed churches ... hold that, in the excepted case, both husband and wife may contract a fresh marriage. (*Pulpit Commentary*, V. 36, p. 96.)

Few people know the historical facts about this divorce question. Some make popish statements about it without having studied it. They do not know that the Eastern Fathers generally were superior theologians and better qualified on the subject than were the Western Fathers.

The Fathers of the Western Church were, as a class, much inferior to those of the Eastern in their exposition of the Scriptures. One chief reason for this fact was their comparative ignorance of the original languages of the Bible. (*Biblical Hermeneutics*, Terry, M. S., p. 41; 1895.)

Another point that disqualified the Western view of the exceptive texts was their strong contempt for marriage. They believed the sexual relations were sinful because of its carnal delight. Children were "born in sin" because of the impurity of the sex act.

The "craze of celibacy" among the Western Fathers influenced them in their divorce teaching of "a mensa et thoro" (separation from bed and board).

With such strong bias, how could they be fair interpreters of the Matthaean exceptions? On the celibacy craze in the early church and the belief that babies were born in sin because of the lust of the sex act, see *The History of Doctrines*, Reinhold Seeberg (2. 173; Baker, 1958); *The History of Sacerdotal Celibacy in the Christian Church*, Henry C. Lea (p. 27, Russel & Russel, 1957).

The *Encyclopaedia Britannica* quotes E. A. Westermarck's *History of Human Marriage* as its authority on the history of marriage and divorce. And Westermarck, in this work, wrote that the separation-from-bed-and-board divorce was rejected—

by nearly all the English reformers of the 16th century as a *popish invention*.

The canonical doctrines that marriage is a sacrament and that it is indissoluble save for death were rejected by the Reformers. They all agreed that divorce, with liberty for the innocent party to remarry, should be granted for adultery, and most of them regarded malicious desertion as a second legitimate cause for the dissolution of marriage. (*History of Human Marriage*, V. 3, p. 334, 1922, Macmillan Co.)

The following five quoted paragraphs were dug up for me by the Research Service of the *Encyclopaedia Britannica*. These researchers quote Dr. T. D. Woolsey who was chairman of the American New Testament committee for revision of the English version of the Bible (1871–81). He was professor of Greek language and literature at Yale University, and also president of Yale (1846–71).

Controversy among the Fathers as to what the grounds should be on which divorce could be allowed was continuous, and *changes were frequent.* The one ground universally accepted was adultery on the part of the wife.

Much as Jerome disparaged marriage, he freely admitted, as did most others, that any number of successive marriages was not unlawful.

Some of the Fathers looked with indulgence on the remarriage of the innocent party.

Nor ought it to be supposed that the Western Church opinion in regard to the lawfulness of remarriage after divorce ran altogether in one direction. The 'leaders of the Church' to whom Origen refers, held that an innocent party might remarry when divorced on account of the adultery of the wife or husband. Lactantius seems to have held the same ... (*Inst.* vi, Sec. 23). So thought also the friend of Augustine, Pollentius. The same thing is taught by Ambrosiaster, as he is called, who is generally thought to be Hilary the Deacon.

An opinion of 1535, signed by Luther, Cruciger, Major, and Melanchthon, allows a woman of Nordhausen, whose husband had absconded several years before, to marry again, according to 'the decision of Paul, and according to the former practice in Christendom, as a similar case cited by Eusebius from Justine, and the example of Fabiola show.' (*Essay on Divorce and Divorce Legislation*, Woolsey, T. D., pp. 103–116, 128–133, Scribner, 1869.)

Augustine is generally considered the greatest theologian among the Latin Fathers. For 15 centuries, his influence throughout the world of Christian theology has been enormous. In early life, he held the no-remarriage view of other Western monks, but after a life-time of study and reflection he had misgivings about the Western opinion. Then Augustine changed his mind, handed down a *Writ of Doubt,* and admitted that the Matthaean exception *could* mean the right to remarriage after divorce for adultery. He wrote:

And in the expressions of the divine word it is so obscure whether he, who has the unquestionable right of putting away an adulterous wife, ought to be accounted an adulterer for taking another, that, as far as I can see, in this case any person may make a pardonable mistake (venialiter ibi quisque fallatur). (*Treatise, de fide et operibus*, iv. 19.)

The New Testament scholar, Dean Alford, quoting Augustine's opinion, wrote:

We may well leave a matter in doubt, of which Augustine could say, that it was so obscure, that error on either side is venial (pardonable).

(*The New Testament for English Readers*,
p. 33.)

If Augustine had interpreted the divorce question
by the same rules that he laid down for the interpretation of other doctrines, there would have been no
doubt in his mind about it. This also goes for Dean
Alford. Scattered through the 1942 pages of his *The
New Testament for English Readers*, I can give 50
references to show that he strongly insisted on the
exact interpretive principles for other doctrines that
we use on the divorce Scriptures. Is it logical to use
these rules on some doctrines but not all?

It is a fair requirement that an interpreter be
consistent with himself, but it is unusual to find one
who is.

John Calvin's reputation as a theologian is respected by many non-Calvin scholars. Even his enemies
admitted he was a brilliant theologian. Calvin taught
that Christ's law against remarriage did not apply to
marriage dissolved for adultery.

> Though Christ condemns as an adulterer the
> man who shall marry a wife that has been di-
> vorced, *this is undoubtedly restricted to unlaw-
> ful and frivolous divorces.* (my emphasis)

> An adulterous wife "cuts herself off as a rotten
> member" of the marriage. It is the "duty of the
> husband to purge his house from infamy." "By
> committing adultery, he (the husband) has dis-
> solved the marriage, the wife is set at liberty."
> (*Harmony of the Evangelists*, Calvin, John,
> V. 2, pp. 383–384.)

The Reformation was a deliverance not only from
the sins of Rome, but also from its unscriptural theo-

logy. The Reformation theologians unitedly rejected Rome's no-remarriage decree. Martin Luther abolished this "popish invention" and wrote:

> But I marvel even more that the Romanists do not allow remarriage of a man separated from his wife by divorce but compel him to remain single. Christ permitted divorce in case of fornication and compelled no one to remain single; and Paul preferred us to marry rather than to burn, and seemed quite prepared to grant that a man may marry another woman in place of the one he has repudiated. (*Reformation Writings of Martin Luther*, Woolf, B. L., p. 307, Lutterworth Press, London, 1952.)

This corroborates Luther's statement in his sermon on marriage at Wittenberg in 1525 that "Matthew 19:9, is a blunt, clear, plain text. . . ."

Melanchthon was another Reformation theologian who rejected the popish non-dissolution decree. He was a distinguished scholar in the doctrinal development of the Reformation period. He was Luther's superior as a scholastic theologian, and Luther respected him greatly.

The Roman Catholic Church has dealt with the divorce texts according to their pleasure. Sometimes these texts mean non-dissolution, and sometimes they don't. The *Encyclopaedia Britannica* researchers also give this information:

> . . . Even under the strictest rules of the Roman Catholic Church, when no divorce was allowed, a way of escape was found. It was laid down that a marriage was indissoluble when it had been 'validly' contracted and consummated. Everything depended on the interpretation of the word

'validly.' Thus though divorce was not allowed, the right to annul the marriage was allowed. And the practice was so universal and so frequent that we find as many as sixteen causes specified for which marriage could be dissolved, while at the same time every care was taken to maintain the fiction of its indissolubility. (This information was taken from *Divorce*, Hartley, C. G., pp. 16, 17, 24, London, 1921.)

I found the following in Philip Schaff's *Creeds of Christendom* (V. 2, p. 229, Harper, 1877):

By the law of nature, the marriage tie is not indissoluble. (*Papal Syllabus of Errors*, 1864.)

It also seems to me that the Archbishop of Canterbury played it two ways. I previously gave you his opinion for dissolution and remarriage on the ground of I Corinthians 7:15. Now get this:

Let me say quite frankly that in some cases where a first marriage has ended in tragedy, a second marriage has, by every test of the presence of the Holy Spirit that we are able to recognize, been abundantly blessed. For this very reason I do not find myself able to *forbid* good people who come to me for advice to embark on a second marriage ... [his italic]. (*Problems of Marriage and Divorce*, Archbishop of Canterbury, Fisher, Geoffrey F., p. 21, Morehouse-Gorham Co., N.Y., 1955.)

Adultery and fornication dissolve the marriage and the innocent party has the right to marry another, as if the offending party were dead. (Westminster Confession. *The Creeds of Chrisendom*, Schaff, Philip, V. 3, p. 656, Harper, 1877.)

The existence of the qualification (except for
fornication) in Matthew indicates that in the
Early Church marriage was allowed to the innocent party. (*Dictionary of the Apostolic
Church.* Editor, James Hastings, V. 1, p. 417,
1908.)

Many Protestant denominations, while upholding
the sanctity of marriage as a basic unit of society,
followed the reformers in their view of dissolution
and remarriage after proven adultery. (See *Encyclopaedia Britannica*, V. 7, p. 514, 1965.)

John Wesley, teacher of logic, and founder of the
Methodist Church, wrote:

It is adultery for any man to marry again . . .
unless that divorce has been for the cause of
adultery; in that only case there is no Scripture
which forbids to marry again. (*A Compend of
Wesley's Theology*, p. 238, Abingdon Press,
1954.)

Here is the testimony of Charles H. Spurgeon:

Marriage is for life, and cannot be loosed, except by the one great crime which severs its
bond . . . a woman divorced for any cause but
adultery, and marrying again, is committing
adultery before God.

Fornication makes the guilty person a fit subject for just and lawful divorce; for it is a
virtual disannulling of the marriage bond. In
a case of fornication, upon clear proof, the tie
can be loosed.

. . . persons once married are in the sight of
God, married for life, with the one exception of

proven fornication. (*Spurgeon's Popular Exposition of Matthew*, pp. 28, 29, 159, 160, Zondervan.)

We conclude that those are in error who claim that for the first five centuries of the Christian Church none of the fathers allowed remarriage after divorce for adultery.

From the bishops that Origen told about in the third century, through the Middle Ages. to Luther, Calvin, Wesley, and Spurgeon, a long and impressive list of great names in Christendom believed that divorce for unfaithfulness dissolved marriage and allowed the right to remarriage.

13

Replies to Objections

Objection 1

I will answer a few of the strongest objections upon which those who deny remarriage after divorce mainly rely. Here is one:

> For the Lord, the God of Israel, saith that he hateth putting away. (Malachi 2:16.)

These words have been used to prove that God is opposed to *all* divorce, and that He hates all divorce. This objection is a distortion. It not only violates the *rule of context*, but also the *rule of text*. Even prominent expositors have lifted these words out of an entire passage and manipulated them to fit their view. The rest of the verse says this:

> ... for one covereth violence with his garment, saith the Lord of hosts; therefore take heed to your spirit, that ye deal not *treacherously*.

And the context says:

> Because the Lord hath been witness between thee and the wife of thy youth, against whom thou hast dealt *treacherously*.
>
> *For* the Lord, the God of Israel, saith that he hateth putting away. (verses 14–16.)

The reader can see that what God hated here was the treachery of these Jews in divorcing innocent wives.

Divorce for adultery is not considered here. This was what Jesus referred to as "hardness of heart" divorce. Three times in verses 14–16 God spoke of their "treacherously" divorcing their wives, but it was not treachery to divorce an adulterous wife.

For centuries in Israel, "just" men had divorced harlot wives and remarried, and God never called that treacherous. God did not hate divorce for adultery and sex perversion. He had such offenders put to death under Moses. Jesus also hates divorce for treachery and hardness of heart, but He does not hate it for fornication.

Objection 2

> For John had said unto Herod, It is not lawful
> for thee to have thy brother's wife. (Mark 6:18.)

This is also used as an argument against all divorce, but it is another distortion because the reason for the unlawfulness of the marriage was clearly stated by John as being "thy brother's wife." John said, "It is not *lawful* for thee. . . . " This was forbidden by the Mosaic law while the brother lived (Lev. 18:16; 20:21). *The Amplified New Testament* lists these two references in connection with this marriage (Matt. 14:4). So also leading commentaries. The question of divorce and remarriage for adultery is not considered in this text. Here again, divorce and remarriage was a question of the lawfulness of Jewish statute.

Objection 3

> A bishop then must be the husband of one wife.
> (I Timothy 3:2.)

Some no-remarriage teachers defend their position with this text. But again, the text does not deal with what objectors make it to mean. *Biblical scholars take different views of this text. Some think that what is forbidden here is polygamy or bigamy. And some monks in the early church were so opposed to marriage that they believed if a man's wife died and he remarried, he was the husband of two wives and was disqualified to be a church officer.

A study of all the facts in this case does not indicate that remarriage after divorce for adultery is considered here. As Christ allowed the right to another marriage after such a divorce we cannot see how this Christ-given right disqualifies a man for the office of elder or deacon. We saw before from Deut. 24:1-4; 1 Cor. 7:15 that after divorce in these cases, the remarried man was recognized by God and the Jewish and Greek courts as the husband of one wife.

We also established from Paul (chapter 11) that after a man was "loosed" from marriage by biblical divorce he was "free" and had "not sinned" in remarriage. Why then should remarriage disqualify him for church office?

> . . . it appears in the highest degree improbable that Paul laid down such a condition (of no second marriage) for the priesthood. There is nothing in his writings when treating expressly of second marriages (Rom. 7:2-3; 1 Cor. 7:8, 39) to suggest the notion of there being anything disreputable in a second marriage, and it would obviously cast a great slur upon second marriage if it were laid down as a principle that no one who had married twice was fit to be an *episkopos* . . . (*Pulpit Commentary*). (This would also apply to second marriage in the cases of divorce in 1 Cor. 7:27-28).

*On this page in previous printings of this book there was an error in a quotation from the *Expositors Greek Testament*, so the quotation has been deleted and the page rewritten.

In the Mosaic divorces, the marriage bond was so completely dissolved that the woman was forbidden to return to the first husband if the second or third husband divorced her (Deut. 24:4).

Objection 4

Turn, O backsliding children, saith the Lord,
for I am married unto you. (Jeremiah 3:14.)

It is argued from this text that divorce does not dissolve marriage because God had given Israel a bill of divorce (3:8), and the divorce did not dissolve the marriage.

Verse 1 refutes this argument. A Jewess, if divorced in the second marriage, could not return to the first husband. The severance of the first bond was complete and final.

In Hebrews 8:9 the apostle referred to the marriage covenant between God and Israel in Jeremiah 31:32, and wrote:

. . . they continued not in my covenant, and I regarded them not, saith the Lord.

"Wilful sin, continued in, means apostasy, repudiation of the covenant" (*Expositors Greek Testament*). "Such a covenant-breaking people could no longer be the subject of covenant mercy on God's part" (Delitzsch, *Commentary on Hebrews*). "The Israelites broke the covenant. Then God annulled it. . . . The covenant was void when they broke it" (Robertson, *Word Studies*, V. 5, p. 392).

Jehovah's covenant of wedlock was made null and void for all Israelites who did not obey its conditions. Most of the Jews with whom God made the covenant will be forever lost. Proof:

Paul, in Romans 9:27, quoted Isaiah concerning the Covenant-Nation:

> Though the number of the children of Israel be as the sand of the sea, a *remnant* shall be saved. (See also 11:5.)

Jesus revealed that all the covenant people would not be saved. He said, "The *children of the kingdom* shall be cast into outer darkness..." (Matt. 8:12). This is eternal darkness. "...to whom is reserved the mist of darkness forever" (II Pet. 2:17). And Jude 6 records: "reserved in everlasting chains under darkness."

Jehovah swore in His wrath that those Israelites who broke the covenant of wedlock with Him would never "enter into my rest" (Heb. 3:11, 18; 4:1–11). The marriage is forever dissolved, and a "great gulf fixed" so that no one can ever "pass" it (Luke 16:26).

I once asked a non-dissolution teacher, who used the above argument from Jeremiah 3:8–14: "Was God married to those Jews who *did not return* to Him?" He did not answer. When I pressed him, he reluctantly admitted his error. Let anyone read the entire book of Jeremiah and he can see that God dissolved His covenant relations with unbelieving Israel by slavery and death at the hands of the Babylonians. But there was always a "remnant" (minority) of faithful ones through whom God continued the covenant.

Objection 5

"If we let down the bars, will there not be much abuse of the remarriage privilege?"

This objection falsely assumes that it is scriptural to have the bars up in the first place. The Scriptures should be dealt with on the basis of what they mean, and not on whether they will be abused. What Bible doctrine or privilege has not been abused?

The privilege of the Fifth Amendment to the U.S. Constitution has been much abused by gangsters and Communists, but there isn't a court or legislature in America that would abolish it.

Why do non-dissolution churches let down the bars and receive divorced and remarried people into their membership when a minister of another denomination performs the ceremony? And why do they let down the bars to receive the tithes and offerings of divorced-remarried persons? Why do they let down the bars to give them right to the Holy Communion? "Consistency is not only a jewel; it is a rare gem."

Objection 6

A denominational editor who read my first book on divorce wrote me this:

> I think you have fairly well established the point you wanted to make. But you did not give any help on the question of how the innocent party can be determined. There no doubt are such, but probably in most marital breakups there has been fault on both sides.

We are not obligated to believe everyone who claims innocence in divorce. We would be foolish if we did. Some claim to be the innocent party who are really the guilty party. Where there is no clear proof, we should not assume innocence.

God believed there were innocent parties in Old Testament times. We saw in Numbers 5:12–31 that when God cursed the guilty wife whose husband suspected her of adultery, the husband was held "guilt-less." Job said adultery was a heinous crime, to be punished by the judges. Moses believed there were innocent parties, because he killed the guilty and set the innocent free. The Holy Spirit said Joseph was a "just man" when he intended to dissolve his marital bond with Mary, as righteous men had done for centuries in Israel after the death penalty was abolished for adultery. Paul believed the Christians in the divorce cases of I Corinthians 7:15 were innocent parties.

Jesus must have believed there were innocent parties or He would not have given us the fornication exception. Surely, He did not give us an unworkable law, even though it may not always be easy to determine who is the innocent party.

In divorce cases in law courts, the evidence for innocence is often convincing. And frequently, contrary to usual procedure, the court gives custody of children to the father. And it has often happened that in the cases of murder for adultery, juries have set the murderer or murderess free.

Should not Christians who claim innocence have right to a hearing before an impartial jury of fellow believers? Paul told the Corinthian church:

> Know ye not that we shall judge angels? how
> much more things that pertain to this life?
> (I Corinthians 6:3.)

In such cases where Christians are concerned, and their fellowship with the church is involved, can they not use the privilege of Matthew 18:17 to "tell it unto the church"? The Holy Spirit gives wisdom and discernment to the body of Christ for such needs (I Cor. 12:8–10).

Pastors, after long experience with their people, usually know who are the innocent parties in divorce, especially when the innocent partner has forgiven an adulterous mate again and again and offered to restore the marriage. And when the adulterous mate rejects all offers of forgiveness and marries another, then the case is different. In marital troubles there is often wrong on both sides; but when one wrong party commits adultery against another wrong party, then the case stands on different ground.

Can they be fair judges who skeptically ask: "*Who is the innocent party?*" To any Christian who claims innocence in divorce, let's give him a fair chance to prove it. Let us give him the same right that a law court gives him. It should not be "trial by prejudice." "Doth *our* law judge any man before it hear him?" (John 7:51). In our marriage counseling, we advise the offended party to forgive the guilty and try to restore their marriage. God has forgiven us as sinners and we should forgive others. But when the offender spurns all offers of mercy and marries another, should not the one who offered the mercy be considered "innocent"?

The main point is to first find out if Christ's divorce law means dissolution; if it does, then He believed there are innocent parties, and He did not give us an unworkable law.

14

Summary of Evidence

1. To show the historical background of the divorce question, we cited nine leading sources on the Hillel-Shammai dispute: Edersheim, Pulpit Commentary, Hastings, Robertson, Jewish Encyclopedia, Universal Jewish Encyclopedia, Lange, Vincent, and the *Encyclopaedia Britannica* authority, E. A. Westermarck. The divorce question was a dispute between rival groups, as was also the question of paying taxes to Caesar. It was not Christ's purpose to take sides in these disputes; but in answering their questions about divorce and taxes, it was an incidental result that His answers upheld one side.

2. We quoted Edersheim, Terry, and others to show that "The Old Testament offers the key to the right interpretation of the New."

3. For 14 centuries, divorce in the Jewish nation, as also among the Gentile nations, had the one and only meaning of dissolution with the right to re-marriage. A separation-divorce was unknown. We went to the origin of the subject in Deuteronomy 24:1–4. Here we found the fact that after a wife was divorced she could "go and be another man's wife." If she was divorced by the second husband, she could marry a third—without being an adulteress. God referred to the first or second husband as her "former husband." If divorce does not dis-

solve marriage, as our opponents claim, then God allowed adulterous remarriage and the illegitimacy of children born in the remarriage. As it is impossible to believe that God allowed adultery, we are forced to the conclusion that the divorce severed the union. This fact destroys the argument that only death can dissolve marriage.

4. Christ approved the Jewish divorce for the cause of fornication. He said, "Whosoever shall put away his wife, saving for the *cause* of fornication. . . ." The Greek for "cause" (logos) means "for which a thing may be *rightly* done." We cited the highest Greek authorities for this definition: Bengel, Thayer, Moulton & Milligan, Arndt & Gingrich, Westcott & Hort lexicons. The case was a matter of rightful cause.

   Christ did not give a Jew the right cause to divorce an adulterous wife and then make it wrong for him to remarry; He did not put a life-long penalty of no-remarriage on the law of right cause.

5. The multitudes who heard Christ hand down His divorce law needed no experts to explain its meaning to them. People sometimes ask: "Why didn't Jesus speak more clearly on divorce and remarriage?" We answer: Understand His divorce law as did the Jews and it will be clear enough.

   Opponents speak of Matthew 5:32 as "an isolated text," but this text was spoken to thousands of "common people." And the law of probability is that they never heard Him speak on the subject again. There was no need for them to hear Him again because the law of 5:32 was a complete statement. It was not left for Paul to clarify it 25 years later in Romans 7. A Jew who heard Christ utter

this "isolated text" could have divorced an unfaithful wife, remarried, and have died before the
Christ-hating Saul of Tarsus was converted.

Christ approved the Jewish divorce for the
cause of fornication. Let all who are confused about
this question accept this fact and they will see
that they no longer have a mystery to unravel.

6. The legal term "put away" had 14 centuries of
grammatical history behind it, and always with
the absolute meaning of dissolution and remarriage.
The writing of divorcement was called *A Bill of
Cutting Off*. We named six Hebrew lexicons and
concordances that give full support to this definition. The non-dissolution teachers have not named
even one for their meaning of "separation." There
are none to name.

7. The Greek word for divorce is the exact equivalent
of the Old Testament word. The primary meaning
is "to set free." We named six leading Greek authorities for this meaning. We proved from Moulton
& Milligan that it had the same sense in papyri
usage. Others have not named one Greek lexicon
for their meaning of separation. There are none
to name.

8. It is a distortion to change the meaning of a Bible
word and give it another meaning not assigned to
it in Scripture.

9. If Christ left any doubt about His meaning of
"put away," can He hold those responsible who
are uncertain about His meaning? *Black's Law
Dictionary* is "the Nations leading law dictionary." Many authorities agree with this work that
says: "Doubtful words will be construed most

strongly against the party using them."

10. On "except it be for fornication," we proved that "except" means "to take out; to exclude from an enumeration, the scope of statement or enactment; to exclude from a number or whole." For this meaning we cited Greek and English dictionaries and top legal sources which give hundreds of citations showing that *except* is understood in this sense in court decisions. Professor A. T. Robertson was cited for the same meaning. Bengel, the Greek authority, was quoted likewise.

Both divorce and remarriage were excepted from the law against putting away. Whether the exception is placed at the beginning, middle, or end of the sentence, the meaning remains the same.

11. We proved that fornication does not signify "premarital sin" only. From Augustine to the *Amplified New Testament*, we showed that fornication has the general sense of unchastity or sexual sin in general. For this definition we quoted various leading Hebrew and Greek lexicons, and cited Moulton & Milligan to show that in papyri usage, fornication was "applied to unlawful sexual intercourse generally." If anything can be established with certainty, it is in the language of the papyri. It was God's purpose to give the New Testament not only to the first-century world, but to all future world generations. And when it passed to the future peoples of the world, it took with it the *native* meaning of the Mediterranean world in which it originated.

We also gave various Old Testament references to prove that fornication was applied to the sexual

sins of married people. Numerous references were
given in the Jewish Apocrypha, early Christian literature, and Classical literature, and many
translations, versions, and revisions, besides eight
English dictionaries and eight Bible dictionaries, and
various New Testament references. There is not
a single proof for the teaching that fornication
refers to premarital sin only.

12. All attempts to prove that the fornication exceptions are not genuine have failed. We quoted the
Catholic Encyclopedia that "the words (except for
fornication) are in general fully vouched for by
the most reliable codices." Matthew's record
stands on ancient manuscript authority.

All the revision committees have retained the
exceptions. When the question came before the
English and American revisers, they deliberately
reaffirmed the text of 1611 and gave us Matthew's
exception in both places. Some scholars who deny
the authenticity of the exceptions admit that, if
genuine. they leave "no doubt that divorce is used
in such sense as covers permission to remarry."
The Westcott-Hort and Nestle texts have the exceptions in both places in Matthew.

13. There is no contradiction between the Gospels because Matthew only has the exceptions. One Gospel
has many details another Gospel does not have. If
each had all the details of the other, there would
be no need for the four of them.

Edersheim, Vincent, Alford, and many scholars agree that "the three synoptic Gospels must
be carefully pieced together. It will be seen that
only thus can they be understood." "An exception
in a fuller account must explain a briefer one."

"The paragraphs containing matter peculiar to Matthew are not fewer than 62." Matthew has "whole blocks of material" peculiar to his Gospel. "Matthew more fully reports." "Matthew has highest rank in the accounts." The reader could see this from the parallel accounts we gave of Matthew and Mark.

As we were interpreting a law, we showed from the legal authorities that a similar rule applies in law courts. "To interpret and reconcile laws so that they harmonize is the best code of construction." "We must collect from the whole one uniform and consistent sense." If this principle is not adopted for scriptural interpretation, how shall we answer those critics who say: "The Bible is self-contradictory"?

14. Opponents ask: "How can all that Jesus taught about marriage be modified with five words (except it be for fornication)?" We reply: How can all that Jesus taught about marriage be modified to allow a separation?

Five words can modify a thousand words. They can (and do) modify whole paragraphs or sections of a law or document. An entire concept of law can be stated in four or five words, as: Except it be for fornication. Thou shalt not kill. Thou shalt not steal. Thou shalt not commit adultery. Thou shalt not covet.

15. When Christ met the Pharisees on divorce in Matthew 19, He answered *their* test question about the lawfulness of it. The subject-matter of this discussion was the Mosaic precedent. Christ did not deny the fact of dissolution in the Deuteronomic statute, but He restricted it to one cause. It had

been *lawful* for every cause; now it was lawful only for one cause.

16. Jesus took His tempters back to the original marriage and showed them the Creator's one-flesh purpose in marriage. But we do not see an adulterous marriage in the beginning. Adam was not an adulterer nor was Eve an adulteress. What Christ told the Pharisees about marriage in the beginning was in reply to their "every cause" question; it does not apply to divorce for adultery.

   Jesus and the Jewish scholars were debating marriage as dissolved by divorce—not marriage as dissolved by death.

   In this passage of Matthew 19:3–9, the term "put away" was used four times, twice by the Pharisees and twice by Jesus. With legal and biblical authorities, it is fundamental to sound interpretation that "a word can have but one fixed meaning in the connection in which it stands." Some false doctrines are violations of this rule.

   In verse 9 of this passage, Jesus allowed a divorce, which, in verse 3, He said was not so from the beginning. This proves that fornication was an exception to all that He taught about marriage. "Except" means *"to exclude from the scope of enactment"*—*"to exclude from an aggregate under consideration."*

17. Jesus did not leave His marriage law to be clarified by Paul 25 years later in Romans 7:1–3.

18. Divorce for adultery is not in view in Romans 7:1–3. The Romans, to whom Paul wrote, knew from the law that when a Jew divorced his wife, she could go and be another man's wife without being

called an adulteress. Dr. Edersheim wrote: "The Jews have it that a woman 'is loosed from her husband' by only one of two things: death or a letter of divorce; hence Rom. 7:2–3." Whether loosed by death or divorce, the marriage was null, void, dead.

19. Jesus said nothing against the death penalty for adultery. And when the divorce bill was substituted for the death penalty, He did not say anything against that. It is true that from the beginning there was no divorce. But it is also true that from the time of Genesis, men killed adulterous wives. There was no need to divorce them when they killed them. Divorce would have been merciful. Christ's law retained the right to "put away evil."

20. The Mosaic writing of divorcement was the nation's official divorce bill. No divorce was legal without it. "Just" men, like Joseph, had used it for centuries to dissolve their marriages to adulterous wives, in both betrothal and completed marriage. Jesus said nothing against this. A Jew could use the bill to divorce an unfaithful wife, then remarry, and still be a righteous man.

21. We submitted top lexical evidence to show that "depart" in I Corinthians 7:10, 11, 15 signified divorce as obtained in the Greek law courts. The believers in verses 10–11 were commanded not to divorce their mates; and if they did, they were to "remain unmarried," or "be reconciled," because there was not valid cause for the divorce, and it did not dissolve the marriage in God's sight. But the "remain *unmarried*" proves that it had been *legally* dissolved, and was recognized as such by the Greek courts.

But in the divorce of verse 15 where the unbeliever divorced the believer, the case was different. Here Paul did not command the believer to
remain unmarried or be reconciled. The believer
was "not under bondage" to the marriage. The Lord
recognized the validity of the Greek divorce in
these cases, as He had accepted the validity of
the Mosaic divorce for fornication. In I Corinthians
7:15, dissolution is decisively expressed in the
term, "not under bondage."

The Greek bill embodied the same severance
of marriage as did the Jewish bill. We quoted the
leading Greek dictionaries for this. "Not under
bondage" signified that the divorced party was no
longer *bound as a slave* to the marriage. This was
sustained by references in Thayer, Arndt & Gingrich, Vine, Abbott-Smith, Westcott & Hort lexicons.

The "remain unmarried" particular of verse
11 was not repeated in verse 15, and *what is not
specified is not required.*

For this view, we gave further testimony from
Vincent, Grotius, 16th and 17th century commentators and reformers, Pulpit Commentary, Hastings, Alford, Lightfoot, Matthew Henry, Expositors
Greek Testament, Church Fathers, Luther, Archbishop of Canterbury, Moffatt's and Wuest's Translations.

The problem of verse 15 is the same today as
when a Jew or Moslem becomes a Christian, and
the unbelieving partner divorces them because of
their faith in Christ. To prevent the divorce, the
believer would have to deny Christ.

22. When there is valid ground for divorce, the marriage is dissolved for both parties. I did not realize
this until it was pointed out to me by Mr. Elmer

Miller, the New York lawyer to whom I have referred. Mr. Miller made a study of the divorce question and concluded that divorce for adultery sets both parties free. He had not realized this himself until he had made his study. I quickly saw his logic. The divorce could not dissolve the union for one without dissolving it for the other. But, the guilty party must take the blame before God for the dissolution of the marriage.

23. Paul, in verse 27, referred to those who had been "loosed" from marriage by divorce. Standard authorities were cited for this fact, and a fact is only as strong as the evidence upon which it is established. Paul then told those that had been loosed (*lusis*) from marriage by divorce: "But if thou marry, thou hast not sinned ... " (v. 28). Those "not under bondage" to their marriages were "loosed" from it. A freed slave was not under bondage to his former master.

24. Some objectors claim there is no support among the church fathers for dissolution, but we proved this false from Augustine, Origen, Eusebius, Pollentius, Ambrosiaster, Lactantius. Also, Luther, Calvin, Melanchthon, Wesley, and Spurgeon. And from Augustine to Spurgeon, there are many more. We cited Hastings, Jamieson, Fausset, & Brown, Encyclopaedia Britannica, and McClintock & Strong. The Eastern Church consistently saw in adultery a legitimate cause of divorce and remarriage. We quoted: " ... at the Council of Trent the Church of Rome forebore to condemn the Eastern discipline on this point."

25. In our replies to objections, we pointed out that a favorite objection was in Malachi where God said

"he hateth putting away." But we showed from
the text and context that God here spoke of Jews
who "treacherously" divorced their wives. Divorce
for adultery is not considered in this text. I have
never known an objector to quote this Scripture
fairly. It was not treachery to divorce an adulterous
wife, or for a wife to divorce an adulterous husband.

26. Some argue from I Timothy 3:2: "A bishop must
be the husband of one wife." We showed that what
was here forbidden was bigamy. We gave various
citations from the *Expositors Greek Testament* to
show that it was also understood in the early
church as referring to bigamy, and that this view
predominates among conservative scholars.

27. Another objection was from Jeremiah 3:14: "Turn,
O backsliding children, for I am married unto you."
The rest of Jeremiah shows that when the
covenant-breaking Jews did not return to Jehovah,
He had them delivered to captivity and death.

28. To the question: "Who is the innocent party?"
we gave various references in both Testaments to
show whom God considered innocent in adulterous
marriage. Adulterous mates were put to death
under Moses. And "just" men used the Mosaic bill
of divorce to dissolve adulterous marriage. *Paul
believed the forsaken believers were innocent in the
cases of divorce in I Corinthians 7:15. Evidently
the unbelievers were satisfied with their marriages
until their mates became Christians, for which
cause they divorced them.* Law courts do not take
the view that there are no innocent parties in
broken marriage. In many cases there is wrong on
both sides; but when one wrong party commits

adultery against another wrong party, the case stands on different ground.

29. The divorce-but-no-remarriage doctrine is a mere begging of the question all the way. It has no proof for its non-dissolution teaching. It is loaded with presumption, and cannot hold its ground when put to the test of proven facts. It sidesteps a logical challenge. There is nothing in its claims that constitutes a basis of proof. It violates all sound rules of interpretation, and if the same method were applied to other doctrines, one could make the Bible mean anything.

It is also a doctrine of inconsistency. Some denominations that hold this doctrine will not allow their ministers to perform a marriage for anyone divorced, but they receive them into the church when the minister of another denomination officiates.

The ministers of non-dissolution denominations are forbidden to perform a marriage for anyone "who has a former companion still living." Here is an illustration. It frequently happens that a married man or woman kills an adulterous mate. When brought to trial, they plead the "unwritten law," and twelve fellow citizens set them free to be married to another. The murderer or murderess can then be remarried by these ministers because when they ask them the usual question: "Do you have a former companion still living?" they can truthfully say no. But, when they caught their mates in adultery, if they had divorced them instead of killing them, they would not have the right to remarriage because—they would have a former companion still living.

30. The reader is familiar with what in civil law is

called *The Law of Reasonable Doubt.* A reasonable doubt is not speculation. It has plausible ground for uncertainty. There may be facts in evidence, which, if unanswered, would cause men of reason to refuse to convict the accused. A lack of sufficient evidence is ground for uncertainty, and this uncertainty will cause men of fairness to hesitate. "A reasonable doubt is one for which a reason can be given."

The non-dissolution teaching must be rejected, not only for insufficient evidence, but for a total lack of it. Could the reader, after viewing the evidence, convict of adultery the proven innocent party who remarries—beyond reasonable doubt?

Across the centuries, the Roman Catholic Church has been the chief exponent of this no-remarriage theology. But to achieve their goal in the ecumenical purpose, they are making surprising changes. It is very likely that they will also change on non-dissolution. They have always had various exceptions to it.

After much study of non-dissolution writers, I can sum up all their arguments with three points:

1. Jesus said, "From the beginning it was not so" (Matt. 19:8).
2. Paul said, "For the woman which hath an husband is bound by the law to her husband as long as he liveth" (Rom. 7:2).
3. In the divorce case of I Corinthians 7:11, Paul told the divorced woman to "remain unmarried."

We have seen much proof to show that all three points are distortions. In Matthew 5:32; 19:9; I Corinthians 7:15, *we gave three exceptions to these three Scriptures* used by our opponents, and *they are the strongest arguments they have.* They stress the general law of marriage, but ignore the exceptions to the general law.

Proof of guilt must be so convincing as to leave not even a *shadow of doubt.* Our innocently divorced brothers and sisters in Christ have been convicted and condemned by this non-dissolution teaching that does not have even a shadow of truth; they have been made moral criminals and their children have been made illegitimate by a non-dissolution doctrine that has never been proved.

I ask the reader to view the evidence and study the facts. "A fact from which an inference can be drawn is evidence." Then, let's remove the cruelty and disgrace that many of our brothers and sisters have suffered because of this unscriptural teaching. Many denominational leaders and pastors allow these divorced people to be received into the membership of their churches, but they will not defend them against the subtle accusation of adultery that continually hangs over them. Should we not do unto them as we would have them do unto us, if our positions were reversed? God save us from the "sin of silence."

There are problems and questions about divorce other than the causes we have dealt with, but we have studied the subject only as far as we could find Scripture and proof to do so. There are some cases of divorce that we cannot deal with because they do not come within the exceptions in Matthew 5:32; 19:9; I Corinthians 7:15. We are often asked questions about some cases of divorce that we cannot answer. This is not a book about *all* divorce cases but about those exceptions that Jesus and Paul gave. Beyond this we cannot go.

Our case rests on the evidence submitted. Biblical divorce dissolves marriage. We close, as we began, with the quote from the noted Bentham:

"Evidence is the basis of justice."

Appendix
Eight Rules of Interpretation

We shall also summarize the rules so the reader can see them together in one place. These rules are the center of all grammatical interpretation. They were developed by specialists in the "science of meaning" over the past 2500 years, from Socrates to the present day. They apply equally to legislative or theological language. Critical analysis is impossible without them. Interpretive scholarship accepts them.

Jesus and the apostles used these rules, and also many prominent fathers of the early church, and also the master theologians of the Middle Ages, to Luther, Wesley, and Calvin, although some were not consistent in their use of them.

When the Emperors Constantine and Justinian tried to settle the doctrinal disputes of their time, they learned that the "word-wars" of the theologians were exceedingly difficult wars to deal with because each word-warrior was determined to make the words mean what he wanted them to mean.

This is true of the twisted mass of doctrinal confusion in Christendom today. All false doctrines, or nearly all, are distortions of biblical words. "The Council of Trent avoided a clear definition of terms" (Seeberg).

"God is not the author of confusion" (I Cor. 14: 33). Who then is the author of these many centuries of confusion about the divorce texts? Who are the authors of all the doctrinal confusion about other texts?

The Bible is a legal document, and throughout the Bible there is frequent use of legal terms and illustrations, and much importance is attached to these legal ideas. The word *Testament* is a legal term, and hundreds of times God spoke of His commandments as "laws." Why then should our interpretation be objected to as "legalistic" when the biblical writers used the contemporary legal language of the Mediterranean world?

The Apostle Peter said, "We have also a more sure word of prophecy ... " and, that no Scripture "is of any private [personal] interpretation" (II Pet. 1:19–20). We cannot have a sure word about the meaning of Scripture or anything unless we have a sure method to interpret the words. Always remember that Satan deceived Eve with *words*.

When two interpretations are claimed for a Scripture, the construction most in agreement with all the facts of the case should be adopted. When all the facts of an interpretation are in agreement they sound together in harmony, like notes in a chord.

Biblical interpretation is more than knowing a set of rules, but it cannot be done without the rules. So, learn the rules, and rightly apply them, and you can disregard what Jerome, the learned Latin father of the Middle Ages, said: "What fools these people be! Everybody thinks he can interpret the Bible."

Solomon said:

A wise man will hear, and will increase learning ... to understand a proverb, and the interpretation. (Proverbs 1:5–6.)

Here are the eight rules:

1. *Rule of Definition*

Any study of Scripture ... must begin with a

study of words. (*Protestant Biblical Interpretation*, Ramm, Bernard, p. 129, W. A. Wilde Co., Boston, 1956.)

Define your terms and then keep to the terms defined. (*The Structural Principles of the Bible*, Marsh, F. E., p. 1, Kregel Publications.)

In the last analysis, our theology finds its solid foundation only in the grammatical sense of Scripture. The interpreter should ... conscientiously abide by the plain meaning of the words. (*Principles of Biblical Interpretation*, Berkhof, pp. 74–75, Baker Book House, 1960.)

The Bible writers could not coin new words since they would not be understood, and were therefore forced to use those already in use. The content of meaning in these words is not to be determined by each individual expositor ... to do so would be a method of interpretation [that is] a most vicious thing. (*Studies in the Vocabulary of the Greek New Testament*, Wuest, Kenneth, pp. 30–37, Eerdmans Pub. Co., 1945.)

[The author] confines the definitions strictly to their literal or idiomatic force; which, after all, will be found to form the best, and indeed the only safe and solid basis for theological deductions of any kind. (*Young's Analytical Concordance*, Prefatory Note.)

2. *Rule of Usage*

The whole Bible may be regarded as written for "the Jew first," and its words and idioms ought

to be rendered according to Hebrew usage.
(*Synonyms of the Old Testament*, Girdlestone,
R. B., p. 14.)

Christ then accepted the usage He found exist-
ing. He did not alter it. (*Pulpit Commentary*,
Matthew, V. 1, xxv, old edition.)

Jesus of Nazareth was a Jew, spoke to and moved
among Jews in Palestine. . . . He spoke first and
directly to the Jews, and His words must have
been intelligible to them. . . It was absolutely
necessary to view that Life and Teaching in
all its surroundings of place, society, popular
life. . . . This would form not only the frame in
which to set the picture of the Christ, but the
very background of the picture itself. (*The Life
and Times of Jesus the Messiah*, Edersheim,
Alfred, V. 1, xii, Eerdmans Pub. Co., 1953.)

In interpreting very many phrases and histories
of the New Testament, it is not so much worth
what we think of them from notions of our
own . . . as in what sense these things were understood by the hearers and lookers on, according
to the usual custom and vulgar dialect of the
nation. (*Bishop Lightfoot*, quoted in *The Vocabulary of the Greek New Testament*, xii, Moulton
& Mulligan, Eerdmans Pub. Co., 1959.)

3. *Rule of Context*

Many a passage of Scripture will not be understood at all without the help afforded by the context; for many a sentence derives all its point
and force from the connection in which it stands.
(*Biblical Hermeneutics*, Terry, M. S., p. 117.
1896.)

[Bible words] must be understood according to the requirements of the context. (*Thayer's Greek-English Lexicon of the New Testament*, p. 97.)

Every word you read must be understood in the light of the words that come before and after it. (*How to Make Sense*, Flesch, Rudolph, p. 51, Harper & Brothers, 1954.)

[Bible words] when used out of context . . . can prove almost anything. [Some interpreters] twist them . . . from a natural to a non-natural sense. (Irenaeus, second-century church father, quoted in *Inspiration and Interpretation*, p. 50, Eerdmans Pub. Co., 1957.)

The meaning must be gathered from the context. (*Encyclopaedia Britannica*, Interpretation of Documents, V. 8, p. 912. 1959.)

4. *Rule of Historical Background*

Even the general reader must be aware that some knowledge of Jewish life and society at the time is requisite for the understanding of the Gospel history. (*The Life and Times of Jesus the Messiah*, Edersheim, Alfred, V. 1, xiii, Eerdmans Pub. Co., 1953.)

The moment the student has in his mind what was in the mind of the author or authors of the Biblical books when these were written, he has interpreted the thought of Scripture. . . . If he adds anything of his own, it is not exegesis. (*International Standard Bible Encyclopedia*, V. 3. p. 1489. 1952.)

Theological interpretation and historical investigation can never be separated from each other.

... The strictest historical ... scrutiny is an in-
dispensable discipline to all Biblical theology. (A
Theological Word Book of the Bible, 30 scholars.
Preface, Macmillan Co., 1958.)

I have said enough to show the part which the
study of history necessarily plays in the intelli-
gent study of the law as it is today. . . . Our only
interest in the past is for the light it throws upon
the present. (U.S. Supreme Court Justice Oliver
Wendell Holmes, Jr., 1902–1932, quoted in *The
World of Law*, V. 2. p. 630. Simon & Schuster.
1960.)

5. *Rule of Logic*

Interpretation is merely logical reasoning. (*Encyclopedia Americana*. V. 15. p. 261. 1953.)

The use of reason in the interpretation of Scripture is everywhere to be assumed. The Bible
comes to us in the forms of human language, and
appeals to our reason ... it invites investigation.
and it is to be interpreted as we interpret any
other volume by a rigid application of the same
laws of language, and the same grammatical
analysis. (*Biblical Hermeneutics*, Terry, M. S.,
p. 25. 1895.)

What is the control we use to weed out false
theological speculation? Certainly the control
is logic and evidence ... interpreters who have
not had the sharpening experience of logic ...
may have improper notions of implication and
evidence. Too frequently such a person uses
a basis of appeal that is a notorious violation of
the laws of logic and evidence. (*Protestant Bib-*

lical Interpretation, Ramm, Bernard, pp. 151–153, W. A. Wilde Co., 1956.)

It is one of the most firmly established principles of law in England and in America that "a law means exactly what it says, and is to be interpreted and enforced exactly as it reads." This is just as good a principle for interpreting the Bible as for interpreting law. (*The Importance and Value of Proper Bible Study*, Torrey, R. A., pp. 67–70, Moody Press, 1921.)

Charles G. Finney, lawyer and theologian, is widely considered the greatest theologian and most successful revivalist since apostolic times. He was often in sharp conflict with the theologians of his day because they violated these rules of interpretation. Finney said he interpreted a Bible passage as he "would have understood the same or like passage in a law book" (*Autobiography*, pp. 42–43).

Finney stressed the need for definition and logic in theology and said the Bible must be understood on "fair principles of interpretation such as would be admitted in a court of justice" (*Systematic Theology*, Preface, ix).

6. *Rule of Precedent*

We must not violate the known usage of a word and invent another for which there is no precedent. (*The Greek New Testament for English Readers*, Alford, Dean. p. 1098, Moody Press.)

The professional ability of lawyers in arguing a question of law, and the judges in deciding it, is thus chiefly occupied with a critical study of

previous cases, in order to determine whether
the previous cases really support some alleged
doctrine. (*Introduction to the Study of Law*,
p. 40, Woodruff, E. H., 1898.)

The first thing he [the judge] does is to compare
the case before him with precedents. . . . Back of
precedents are the basic judicial conceptions
which are postulates of judicial reasoning, and
farther back are the habits of life, the institutions
of society, in which those conceptions had their
origin. . . . Precedents have so covered the ground
that they fix the point of departure from which
the labor of the judge begins. Almost invariably,
his first step is to examine and compare them. It
is a process of search, comparison, and little
more. (U.S. Supreme Court Justice Benjamin
Cardozo, 1932–1938, *The Nature of the Judicial
Process*, quoted in *The World of Law*, V. 2,
p. 671, Simon & Schuster, 1960.)

7. *Rule of Unity*

[It is] fundamental to a true interpretation of
the Scripture, viz., that the parts of a document,
law, or instrument are to be construed with reference to the significance of the whole. (Dean
Abbot, *Commentary on Matthew*, Interpretation, p. 31.)

Where a transaction is carried out by means
of several documents so that together they form
part of a single whole, these documents are read
together as one. . . . [They are to be so read]
that, that construction is to be preferred which

will render them consistent. (*Interpretation of Documents*, Sir Roland Burrows, p. 49, Lutterworth & Co., London, 1946.)

8. *Rule of Inference*

In the law of evidence, an inference is a fact reasonably implied from another fact. It is a logical consequence. It is a process of reasoning. It derives a conclusion from a given fact or premise. It is the deduction of one proposition from another proposition. It is a conclusion drawn from evidence. An inferential fact or proposition, although not expressly stated, is sufficient to bind. This principle of interpretation is upheld by law courts. (Jesus proved the resurrection of the dead to the unbelieving Sadducees by this rule (Matt. 22:31, 32). *See Encyclopaedia Britannica*, V. 6, p. 615 (1952) and *Black's Law Dictionary*, p. 436, Fourth Edition, West Pub. Co., 1951.)

A proposition of fact is proved when its truth is established by competent and satisfactory evidence. By competent evidence is meant such evidence as the nature of the thing to be proved admits. By satisfactory evidence is meant that amount of proof which ordinarily satisfies an unprejudiced mind beyond reasonable doubt. Scripture facts are therefore proved when they are established by that kind and degree of evidence which would in the affairs of ordinary life satisfy the mind and conscience of a common man. When we have this kind and degree of evidence it is unreasonable to require more. (*Systematic Theology*, Strong, Augustus H., p. 142, Judson Press, 1899.)

It would have been easy to quote many more Biblical and legal authorities on interpretation and evidence, but it would have been needless repetition.

General Bibliography

Abbott, Lyman, *The Gospel According to Matthew*, "Interpretation," A. S. Barnes Co., 1878.

Abbot-Smith, G., *A Manual Greek Lexicon of the New Testament*, New York: Charles Scribner's Sons, undated.

Alford, Henry, *The New Testament for English Readers*, Chicago: Moody Press, undated.

American Jurisprudence, law encyclopedia, San Francisco: Bancroft & Whitney Co., 1940.

Amplified New Testament, Grand Rapids: Zondervan Publishing Co., 1958.

Amplified Old Testament, Zondervan Publishing Co., 1962.

Antiquities of the Christian Church, Editor, Joseph Bingham, London: Reeves & Turner, 1878.

Arndt, Wm. F. and Gingrich, F. W., *A Greek English Lexicon of the New Testament*, Chicago: University of Chicago Press, 1957.

Augustine, Treatise, *de fide et operibus*, iv. 19.

Baker's Dictionary of Theology, Editor, Everett N. Harrison, Grand Rapids: Baker Book House, 1960.

Bengel, Johann, *Gnomon of the New Testament*, V. 1, 1860.

Berkhof, L., *Principles of Biblical Interpretation*, Grand Rapids: Baker Book House, 1960.

Black, H. C., *Black's Law Dictionary*, St. Paul: West Publishing Co., 1951.

Broom, Herbert, *Principles of Legal Interpretation*, Sweet & Maxwell, Ltd., London, 1937.

Bryant, M. M., *English in the Law Courts—The Part that Articles, Prepositions and Conjunctions Play in Legal Decisions*, New York: Frederick Ungar Publishing Co., 1962.

Burrows, Sir Roland, *Interpretation of Documents*, London: Lutterworth & Co., 1946.

Calvin, John, *Harmony of the Evangelists*, 3 vols., Grand Rapids: Eerdmans Publishing Co., Reprint, 1948.

Cardoza, Benjamin, "The Nature of the Judicial Process," in *The World of Law*, 2 vols., Editor, Ephraim London, New York: Simon & Schuster, First Printing, 1960.

Catholic Encyclopedia, "Divorce," V. 5, New York: Robert Appleton Co., 1913.

Charles, R. H., *The Teaching of the New Testament on Divorce*, Williams & Norgate, London, 1921.

Companion to the Bible, a dictionary of the major theological terms and ideas found in the Bible, 37 authors, Editor, Von Allmen, J.J., New York: Oxford University Press, 1958.

Compend of Wesley's Theology, edited by Robert W. Burtner and Robert E. Chiles, Nashville: Abingdon Press, 1954.

Corpus Juris Secundum, law encyclopedia, V. 48, p. 112, New York: American Law Book Co., 1947.

Cyclopedic Law Dictionary, p. 411, Third Edition, Chicago: Callahan & Co.

Dana, H. B. and Mantey, Julius R., *A Manual Grammar of the Greek New Testament,* 25th edition, New York: The Macmillan Co., 1960.

Deissmann, Adolph, *Light from the Ancient East,* The New Testament illustrated by recently discovered texts of the Graeco-Roman world. Translated by Lionel R. M. Strachan. Reprint. Grand Rapids: Baker Book House, 1965.

Dictionary of the Apostolic Church, Editor, Hastings, James, V. 1, p. 417, New York: Charles Scribner's Sons, 1908.

Dictionary of Christ and the Gospels, Editor, Hastings, James, V. 1, p. 484, New York, Charles Scribner's Sons, 1906.

Edersheim, Alfred, *The Life and Times of Jesus the Messiah,* 2 vols., Grand Rapids: Wm. B. Eerdmans Co., 1953.

———, *Sketches of Jewish Social Life,* Wm. B. Eerdmans Co., 1957.

Encyclopedia Americana, "Interpretation," V. 15, p. 265, 1958.

Encyclopaedia Britannica, "Interpretation of Documents," V. 7, p. 514, 1965; V. 6, p. 615, 1952.

Encyclopedia of Religion & Ethics, V. 8, p. 438, Editor, Hastings, James, Charles Scribner's Sons, 1951.

Expositors Greek Testament, Editor, Nicoll, W. Robertson, 5 vols., Grand Rapids: Wm. B. Eerdmans Publishing Co., 1956.

Fairbairn, Patrick, *The Typology of Scripture,* Reprint. Grand Rapids: Zondervan Publishing House, undated.

Farrar, Frederic W., *History of Interpretation,* Baker Book House, 1961.

Flesch, Rudolph, *How To Make Sense,* New York: Harper & Bro., 1954.

Finney, Charles G., *Autobiography,* Fleming H. Revell Co., undated.

———, *Systematic Theology,* South Gate, Calif.: Colporteur Kemp, undated.

Fisher, Geoffrey, *Problems of Divorce and Remarriage,* New York: Morehouse & Gorman Co., 1955.

Girdlestone, R. B., *Synonyms of the Old Testament—Their Bearing on Christian Doctrine,* Grand Rapids: Wm. B. Eerdmans Co., undated.

Goodman, Philip and Hanna, *Jewish Marriage Anthology,* Philadelphia: Jewish Publication Society, 1965.

Gore, Charles, *The Question of Divorce,* London, 1911.

Greenleaf, Simon, *Testimony of the Evangelists Examined by Evidence Administered in Courts of Law,* 1874.

Hartley, C. G., *Divorce,* London, 1921.

Hebrew & English Lexicon of the Old Testament, Brown, Driver, & Briggs, Boston: Houghton, Mifflin & Co., 1906.

Henry, Matthew, *Commentary on the Whole Bible,* New York: Fleming H. Revell Co., 6 vols., undated.

Holmes, Oliver Wendell, Jr., "The Path of the Law," in *The World of Law,* V. 2, p. 630, Editor, London, Ephraim, New York: Simon Schuster, 1960.

International Standard Bible Encyclopedia, Editor, Orr, James, 5 vols., Grand Rapids, Wm. B. Eerdmans Co., 1952.

Inspiration and Interpretation, Editor, Walvoord, John F., Grand Rapids: Wm. B. Eerdmans Co., First Printing, 1957.

Jamieson, Fausset, & Brown, *A Commentary, Critical, Experimental and Practical on the Old and New Testaments,* 6 vols., Grand Rapids: Wm. B. Eerdmans Co., 1945.

Jewish Encyclopedia, V. 44, New York: Funk & Wagnalls Co., 1916.

Josephus Historical Works, New and Complete Edition, Tr., William Whiston, Philadelphia: Henry T. Coates & Co., undated.

Kent, C. F., *Israel's Laws and Legal Precedents,* New York: Charles Scribner's Sons, 1907.

Lea, Henry C., *The History of Sacerdotal Celibacy in the Christian Church,* New York: Russell & Russell Co., 1957.

Lightfoot, J. B., *Notes on the Epistles of Paul,* Grand Rapids: Zondervan Publishing House, 1957.

Liddell, Henry George and Scott, Robert, *A Greek English Lexicon,* Oxford: At the Clarendon Press, 1940.

Marsh, F. E., *The Structural Principles of the Bible,* Grand Rapids: Kregel Publications, undated.

Masoretic Text, *The Holy Scriptures According to the Masoretic Text,* Philadelphia: Jewish Publication Society, 1955.

McClintock-Strong Encyclopedia, 12 vols., 1878.

McCormick, Charles T., *Handbook of the Law of Evidence,* Hornbook Series, St. Paul: West Publishing Co., 1954.

Moffat, James, *The Holy Bible,* A New Translation by James Moffatt, New York: Harper & Brothers, 1926.

Morgan, G. Campbell, *The Gospel According to Matthew,* New York: Fleming H. Revell Co., 1929.

————, *The Parables and Metaphors of Our Lord,* Fleming H. Revell Co., 1943.

Moulton, James Hope and Milligan, George, *The Vocabulary of the Greek New Testament,* Illustrated from the Papyri and Other Non-Literary Sources, Grand Rapids: Wm. B. Eerdmans Co., 1949.

Murray, John, *Divorce*, Philadelphia: Westminster Press, 1953.

Neander, Johann, in *Essay on Divorce and Divorce Legislation*, Woolsey, T. D., New York: Scribner's, 1869.

Nestle, D. Eberhard and Nestle, D. Ervin, *Novum Testamentum Graece*, Privileg. Wurtt. Bibelanstalt Stuttgart, 1960.

New Century Dictionary, edited by H. G. Emery and K. G. Brewster, New York: Appleton-Century-Crofts, Inc.

New Testament in Greek, Lexicon, Westcott & Hort, New York: The Macmillan Company, 1953.

Patristic Greek Lexicon, edited by G. W. H. Lampe, 5 vols., New York: Oxford University Press, 1961.

Pope Legal Definitions, Chicago: Callahan & Co., 1919.

Pulpit Commentary, 52 volumes, New York: Funk & Wagnalls Co., undated.

Revelation and the Bible, edited by Carl F. H. Henry, Grand Rapids: Baker Book House, First Printing, 1958.

Robertson, A. T., *A Grammar of the Greek New Testament in the Light of Historical Research*, Nashville: Broadman Press, 1934.

————, *Word Pictures in the New Testament*, 6 volumes, Nashville: Broadman Press, Ninth Printing, 1933.

Schaff, Philip, *Creeds of Christendom*, 3 volumes, New York: Harper, 1877.

Scofield Reference Bible, New York: Oxford University Press, 1917.

Seeburg, Reinhold, *Textbook of the History of Doctrines*, Grand Rapids, Baker Book House, 1958.

Sophocles, E. A., *A Greek Lexicon of the Roman and Byzantine Periods*, New York: Scribner's & Sons, 1887.

Spurgeon, Charles H., *Popular Exposition of Matthew*, Zondervan Pub. House.

Stammler, Rudolph, *The Theory of Justice*, New York: Macmillan Co., 1925.

Strong, Augustus, *Systematic Theology*, Philadelphia: Judson Press, 1899.

Strong, James, *The Exhaustive Concordance of the Bible*, New York: Abingdon Cokesbury Press, 1947.

Student's Hebrew Lexicon, edited by Davies, Benjamin and Mitchell, Edward C., Grand Rapids: Kregel Publications, 1957.

Suplee, T. D., *Trench on Words*, New York: A. C. Armstrong & Son, 1896.

Terry, M. S., *Biblical Hermeneutics*, New York: Hunt & Eaton, 1895.

Thayer, J. H., *A Greek English Lexicon of the New Testament*, American Book Company, 1889.

Theological Word Book of the Bible, edited by Alan Richardson, New York: The Macmillan Company, Seventh Printing, 1958.

Thorndike-Barnhart High School Dictionary, Chicago: Scott, Foresman and Company, 1952.

Torah, The, The Five Books of Moses, Philadelphia: Jewish Publication Society, 1962.

Torrey, R. A., *The Importance and Value of Proper Bible Study,* Chicago: Moody Press, 1921.

Tracy, John Evarts, *Handbook of the Law of Evidence,* New York: Prentice-Hall, Inc., 1952.

Trench, R. C., *Notes on the Parables of Our Lord,* New York: D. Appleton and Company, 1890.

Twentieth Century Encyclopedia of Religious Knowledge, 2 volumes, Grand Rapids: Baker Book House, 1955.

Universal Jewish Encyclopedia, V. 3, New York: The Universal Jewish Encyclopedia, Inc., 1941.

Vincent, M. R., *Word Studies in the New Testament,* 4 volumes, Grand Rapids: Wm. B. Eerdmans Company, 1957.

Vine, W. E., *Expository Dictionary of New Testament Words,* 4 volumes, London: Oliphants Ltd., 1948.

Webster's Third New International Dictionary, G. & C. Merrian Co., 1961.

Westermarck, E. A., *History of Human Marriage,* 3 volumes, New York: The Macmillan Co., 1922.

————, *A Short History of Human Marriage,* New York: The Macmillan Company.

Weymouth, R. F., *The New Testament in Modern Speech,* Boston: The Pilgrim Press, 1937.

Wigmore, John H., *Wigmore on Evidence,* A Student's Textbook of the Law of Evidence, New York: The Foundation Press, Inc., 1935.

Woodruff, Edwin H., *Introduction to the Study of Law,* New York: Baker, Voorhis & Company, 1898.

Woolsey, T. D., *Essay on Divorce and Divorce Legislation,* New York: Scribner's, 1869.

Words and Phrases, law encyclopedia, 101 volumes, St. Paul: West Publishing Company, 1950.

Wuest, Kenneth, *Studies in the Vocabulary of the Greek New Testament,* Grand Rapids: Eerdmans Publishing Company, 1945.

Young, Robert, *Analytical Concordance to the Bible,* Twentieth American Edition, New York: Funk & Wagnalls Company.

————, *Young's Literal Translation of the Bible,* Revised Edition, Grand Rapids: Baker Book House, 1956.